THE BEST OF NEW YORK IN 6 WALKS

WALK **1** > DUMBO, WALL STREET, CHINATOWN & LOWER EAST SIDE p. 18

In the hip neighborhood of Dumbo, warehouses have come to new use. Many of the city's roots lie in historic Wall Street. Chinatown is filled with unique shopping experiences, and in the Lower East Side you'll find trendy boutiques and popular restaurants.

WALK **2** > NOLITA, SOHO, WEST VILLAGE & HIGH LINE p. 38

This route goes through the heart of the city. You'll find galleries and boutiques in SoHo, a bohemian vibe in the West Village, and trendy shops and bars in NoLIta. Head up to the High Line and enjoy the view from above.

WALK **3** > TIMES SQUARE & UNION SQUARE p. 58

From Rockefeller Center and Times Square to MoMA and the Empire State Building, this route will take you past some of the best-known spots in NYC. Plus, there's shopping on 5th Avenue, of course.

WALK **4** > UPPER EAST SIDE & CENTRAL PARK p. 78

Escape the bustle of the city on the streets of the Upper East Side. This walk includes Central Park and all the main museums in the eastern part of the city.

WALK **5** > UPPER WEST SIDE & HARLEM p. 98

Walk along the Hudson River through some of NYC's lesser-known recreational areas, visit Columbia University, and learn about the history of jazz and African American culture in Harlem.

WALK **6** > WILLIAMSBURG p. 118

Tucked in among the warehouses on the East River you'll find popular cafés, amazing coffee shops, and trendy secondhand stores. Williamsburg is home to many artists and hipsters.

MOON NEW YORK CITY WALKS

Step off the plane and head toward the newest, hippest café in town. Find out where to get the best fish in the city or where there is locally brewed beer on tap. Local authors share with you only genuine highlights of the city they love. This way, you can skip the busy shopping streets and just stroll through the city at your own pace, taking in a local attraction on your way to the latest and greatest concept stores. Savor every second and make your city trip a truly feel-good experience.

NEW YORK BOUND!

The Big Apple may be known for its skyscrapers, yellow taxicabs, and famous places such as Times Square, the Guggenheim, the 9/11 Memorial, and Central Park, but it's the many diverse neighborhoods—each with its own distinct character and vibe—that make New York such an inspiring city. From exotic Chinatown and trendy SoHo to the nocturnal West Village and creative Williamsburg, NYC has a place that's perfect for everyone. Want to know the best spots to go in each part of the city? We'll show you.

ABOUT THIS BOOK

Moon New York City Walks lets you discover the city by foot and at your own pace, so you can relax and experience the local lifestyle without having to do a lot of preparation beforehand. Our walks take you past our favorite restaurants, cafés, museums, galleries, shops, and other notable attractions—places in our city we ourselves like to go to and that we really enjoy. So who knows, you might even run into us.

None of the places mentioned here have paid to appear in either the text or the photos, and all text has been written by an independent editorial staff.

DEC - - 2020

CITY
NEW YORK

WORK & ACTIVITIES
**RESTAURANT
PASTRY CHEF
AND
PRIVATE CHEF**

LOCAL
TED STEINEBACH

Ted worked as a pastry chef in one of the best restaurants in New York and the world. Now he has some more time on his hands, and he follows his passions: cooking and eating! He loves to share his tips for New York, so you get to enjoy this amazing city as much as he does.

PRACTICAL INFORMATION

The six walks in this book allow you to discover the funnest neighborhoods in the city by foot and at your own pace. The routes will take you past museums and notable attractions, but more importantly they'll show you where to go for good food, drinks, shopping, entertainment, and an overall good time. Check out the map at the front of this book to see which areas of the city the walks will take you through.

Each route is clearly indicated on a detailed map at the beginning of the relevant chapter. The map also specifies where each place mentioned is located. The color of the number lets you know what type of venue it is (see the key at the bottom of this page). A description of each place is then given later in the chapter.

Without taking into consideration extended stops at any one location, each walk will take a maximum of three hours. The approximate distance is indicated at the top of the page, before the directions.

GOOD TO KNOW

New Yorkers love eating out. Maybe this is because the average kitchen in a New York City apartment is incredibly small. Whatever the reason, there are nearly 20,000 restaurants to choose from.

Most New Yorkers eat dinner between 7pm and 9pm. Reservations often aren't necessary, although at really popular restaurants you may have to wait awhile for a table. At more upscale restaurants, however, reservations are required for lunch as well as for dinner. When in doubt, call ahead to be sure.

LEGEND

● >> SIGHTS & ATTRACTIONS   ● >> SHOPPING
● >> FOOD & DRINK   ● >> MORE TO EXPLORE
☼ >> WALK HIGHLIGHT

When you get your bill, you'll notice the sales tax has been added. In New York, there is an 8.875 percent tax on all restaurant meals. Since a tip of 15-20 percent is expected, a handy rule of thumb for those who don't want to bother with the math is to simply double the sales tax to know how much to tip. Regardless of the quality of the service, always tip your servers and bartenders—they rely on tips as part of their income. Be aware that if you are with a group of five or more, a 20 percent gratuity is automatically added to the bill in many restaurants. Always read the fine print on the menu and, especially when you're with a large group, check your bill closely before you pay to make sure you don't tip twice.

Sales tax on clothes and shoes is 4.5 percent, and this generally is not included in the price tag. For other products, such as cosmetics and household items, the sales tax is 8.8 percent. For hotel rooms, tax is 14.75 percent.

FESTIVALS & EVENTS
Something's always going on in New York. Notable events include:

Usually in February > Lunar New Year Parade
March 17 > St. Patrick's Day Parade
Late June > Coney Island Mermaid Parade
Last weekend in June > NYC Pride March
Second Sunday in June > Puerto Rican Day Parade
October 31 > Village Halloween Parade
Early November > New York City Marathon
Fourth Thursday in November > Macy's Thanksgiving Day Parade
Late November-late December > Christmas at Rockefeller Center
December 31 > New Year's Eve at Times Square

PUBLIC HOLIDAYS
In addition to days that don't fall on a specific date, such as Good Friday, the following are official holidays in the United States:

New Year's Day > January 1
Martin Luther King Jr. Day > third Monday in January
President's Day > third Monday in February
Memorial Day > last Monday in May
Independence Day > July 4

Labor Day > first Monday in September
Columbus Day > second Monday in October
Veterans Day > November 11
Thanksgiving > fourth Thursday in November
Christmas > December 25

HAVE ANY TIPS?

We've put a lot of care into writing this guidebook. Yet shops and restaurants in New York come and go fairly regularly. We do our best to keep the walks and contact details as up to date as possible and to update the print edition as often as we can. However, if despite our best efforts there is a place that you can't find, or if you have any other comments or tips about this book, then let us know. Email us at info@momedia.nl.

TRANSPORTATION

The most direct way to get to and from the airport is by taxi. A trip from **John F. Kennedy (JFK) Airport** to Manhattan will take you between 40 minutes and one hour, depending on traffic, for a set rate of $52.50 (plus toll). Rides from JFK to other parts of the city will cost you between $38 and $65. If you're coming in through **Newark,** New Jersey, you can also expect it to take 40 minutes to one hour to get into the city, and the taxi ride will cost you between $50 and $75 (plus toll). If you're flying into **LaGuardia** in Queens, it will take you about 20-40 minutes to get into Manhattan and will cost you between $20 and $35. Don't forget to factor in the tip—it is customary to tip taxi drivers 15-20 percent.

A less expensive alternative is to take a **shuttle,** such as New York Airport Service Express (www.nyairportservice.com), Olympia Airport Express (www.olympiabus .com), or SuperShuttle (www.supershuttle.com). Shuttles cost between $12 and $23 per person.

It's also possible to get from the airport into the city using public transportation. **Bus M60** from LaGuardia will take you into Manhattan. From Newark, the AirTrain will get you to Penn Station in Midtown in 45 minutes for $12. And from JFK, the AirTrain will bring you to the E train, which you can take into the city.

Once you are in the city, the fastest way to get around is by **subway.** Generally speaking, the subway is clean and safe, provided—of course—you don't go around conspicuously flaunting all your valuables. To use the subway, you need a MetroCard. These are available in SingleRide tickets ($2.75), Pay-Per-Ride cards, or Unlimited Ride cards for specific durations of time. Pay-per-ride cards work with a balance (maximum $80), and you get bonus credit when you put $10 or more on your card. The Unlimited Ride cards come in two options: 7-day unlimited rides ($31) or 30-day unlimited rides ($116.50). During this period, you can use your card as much as you want but only once every 18 minutes and for one person at a time.

Subways stops are named—simply enough—after the street where they're located. Some stations have convenient separate entrances for trains heading north (uptown) and those heading south (downtown). At every station, you'll find a map of the subway and any special service notices. This is also all available at www.mta.info.

There are also plenty of **taxis** in NYC. Just stick your hand out and one will soon stop for you. Taxis are available when the number on top is illuminated. When the words "off duty" are lit up, the driver isn't picking up customers, and when no light is on, the taxi is occupied. When telling the driver where you want to go, it's handy if you also know the cross streets (for example, 52nd Street, between 1st and 2nd avenues).

Taxis can carry a maximum of four passengers, and the average price for a 3-mile ride is $7-11, depending on the traffic and time of day. For such a journey, the tip should be about $1—for longer rides it should be 15-20 percent. You can pay for a cab in cash or with credit card. When you pay with card, the machine itself will suggest a tip for you. When you leave the cab, always ask for the receipt. It has the taxi number on it, which is convenient to have if there is a problem or if you accidentally leave something behind.

BIKING

In recent years, bikes have become an increasingly popular way to explore New York City. Since the city continues to create new bike lanes, more and more New Yorkers have been hopping on the saddle. Traffic may be chaotic, but biking is a trend that's here to stay. The most popular bike routes are through Central Park, over the Brooklyn Bridge, along the Brooklyn Esplanade, next to the Hudson River, and through the eastern part of Manhattan.

Citi Bike (www.citibikenyc.com) is NYC's bike share program, which anyone can use. There are hundreds of stations around the city where you can borrow a bike. After you're done, simply return it to any other station for the next person to use. Bikes are available for 30-minute increments, which can be extended to 60 minutes for an additional fee. You can also opt for a day pass ($10) or a one-week pass ($25). After paying, be sure to immediately put away your credit card before continuing with your transaction. For long journeys, it may be a better idea to rent a bike through a bike rental or bike shop, which will cost about $8-10 for two hours. If you choose to go this route, reserve your bike or tour online beforehand to guarantee you get a bike or spot on the tour—particularly during the summer. Reservations can be made online, for example, using the website bikenewyorkcity.com.

Need a break from the city that never sleeps? Then take a bike ride along the Hudson River. Start in the West Village at the Waterfront Bicycle Shop (www.bikeshopny.com) or book a tour through Rolling Orange Bike Tours (rollingorangebikes.com).

New York City traffic can be particularly hectic. Bike lanes are usually on the left-hand side of the road and sometimes continue on the opposite side of the street. Not all drivers are accustomed to the significant increase in two-wheel traffic, so always remain alert and don't forget to rent a helmet with your bike. The most important traffic rules to remember are that pedestrians have the right of way, riding on the sidewalk is not allowed, cyclists must ride in the same direction as traffic, and traffic lights and signs apply to bikes the same way they do to cars. Traffic rules are strictly enforced and the fines for breaking them are hefty.

For more information about cycling in New York City, visit www.nycgo.com /articles/bike-itineraries.

| TOP 10 | **ARTS & CULTURE** |

1 Enjoy a shot at **Double Dutch Espresso** > p. 113

2 **Partners Coffee** serves a delicious brew > p. 126

3 Good and fair trade is the philosophy at **Prodigy Coffee** > p. 49

4 Grab a cup on the go at **Saturdays Surf** > p. 53

5 **Hungarian Pastry Shop** is a college haunt > p. 111

6 **Stumptown Coffee Roasters** is at the Ace Hotel > 18 W 29th St

7 **Little Collins** has the best espresso > p. 70

8 Sip in **Bakeri**'s backyard garden > p. 126

9 **Butterfield Market** is an area favorite > p. 90

10 **Rabbithole Restaurant** is perfection > p. 125

TOBY'S ESTATE

TOP 10 NIGHTLIFE

1 Hear great bands at **Arlene's Grocery** > p. 37

2 **Radegast Hall & Biergarten** is authentic > p. 125

3 **The Press Lounge** has a big rooftop bar > 653 11th Ave

4 **Angel's Share** serves unique cocktails > 8 Stuyvesant St

5 Jam out to jazz at **Café Carlyle** > p. 97

6 Fun comedians are at **Upright Citizens Brigade Theatre** > p. 142

7 **The Bedford** makes for a relaxed night out > p. 129

8 **Fat Cat** is no-nonsense jazz and beer > 75 Christopher St

9 **Boom Boom Room** is upscale > 848 Washington St

10 Punk, pop, rock, and funk at **Knitting Factory** > p. 134

WALK 1

DUMBO, WALL STREET, CHINATOWN & LOWER EAST SIDE

ABOUT THE WALK

This walk takes you down Dumbo and Wall Street—historic parts of New York. You'll also explore the Lower East Side, where young, creative professionals go for the trendy shops and popular restaurants. Finally, the route will take you to Chinatown, a neighborhood that attracts young residents thanks to low rents. It's also great for the amazing, exotic food that won't break the bank.

THE NEIGHBORHOODS

Until recently **Dumbo** (Down Under Manhattan Bridge) was a ferry port, full of warehouses and commercial buildings. At the end of the 20th century the entire neighborhood was bought by David Walentas, which started a revival, and hip tech startups moved in.

Up until the 19th century, life in New York City was primarily concentrated in what is now Lower Manhattan. Around 1700, the city barely extended beyond Fulton Street, and 100 years later only a handful of additional apartment blocks had been built. When **City Hall** opened in 1812 it seemed unimaginable that the city might continue growing to the north. This historic area is rich with beautiful buildings that date back to some of the city's earliest days—from the imposing Gregorian- and Federal-style architecture around **Wall Street,** to the apartment buildings and temples in Chinatown.

At the end of the 19th century, **Chinatown** was often the scene for fighting street gangs, such as the Dead Rabbits and the Bowery Boys. Apartments in what is today **Columbus Park** garnered notorious nicknames such as Bone Alley, Kerosene Row, and Bandits' Roost. However, Chinatown has long-since shaken off this negative reputation. Today the dynamic neighborhood is a popular destination, thanks to its plethora of stores and restaurants.

Some 200 years ago the **Lower East Side** was flooded with immigrants, and the **Lower East Side Tenement Museum** on Orchard Street is an excellent place to gain insight into the history of the neighborhood. Today many young people are attracted to the happening (night) scene and trendy bars, cafés, and boutiques. With its numerous galleries, the neighborhood also appeals to art aficionados. When walking around, don't forget to look up from time to time to see the beautiful brick buildings with those great fire escapes that are so characteristic of New York City.

SHORT ON TIME? HERE ARE THE HIGHLIGHTS:
6 STATEN ISLAND FERRY + 12 SCHILLING + 14 9/11 MEMORIAL MUSEUM + 15 CENTURY 21 + 18 BROOKLYN BRIDGE

TIPS
// Weekdays are the best time to explore historic Wall Street
// The Lower East Side is nicest at the end of the day or on the weekend
// The last part of the route is perfect for biking

DUMBO, WALL STREET, CHINATOWN & LOWER EAST SIDE

WALK 6

LEGEND

» SIGHTS & ATTRACTIONS

» FOOD & DRINK

» SHOPPING

» MORE TO EXPLORE

» WALK HIGHLIGHT

0   0.25 m
0   0.25 km

Subway Line ⌐ *Times Square*
A-C-E Ⓜ ⌐ Station Name

© MOON.COM

WALK 1 DESCRIPTION (approx. 6.8 mi/11 km)

Start with a beautiful view ❶. Walk through Pearl Street and take the first left for a concept store ❷. Go underneath the bridge and take a left onto Main Street for cookies ❸. Go right onto Water Street and take a ride on the carousel ❹. Continue underneath the Brooklyn Bridge to Brooklyn Park for the ferry ❺. From Staten Island Ferry terminal ❻, go left into Battery Park and then walk right along the water to visit the castle ❼. On the other side of the park, check out the museum ❽. Then turn right on Whitehall Street and left on Bridge Street. Visit Fraunces Tavern ❾ or take a left onto Broad Street. Turn right on William Street and right again on Coenties Alley. The first left is Stone Street ❿. Take a left on Williams Street and left again onto Wall Street for more sightseeing ⓫. On Broadway take a left and an immediate right onto Rector Street and have a schnitzel on Washington Street ⓬. Walk one block to get to Trinity Church ⓭ and follow along to get to Trinity Place. Turn left onto Liberty Street to visit the 9/11 Memorial Museum ⓮. From Greenwich Street, take a right on Dey Street for shopping ⓯, then turn left for a chapel ⓰. Walk along Broadway until you see New York City Hall ⓱ on your right. Walk through the park and go left for the Brooklyn Bridge ⓲, the Municipal Building ⓳, and the CityStore ⓴. Continue on Centre Street to Worth Street and turn right. Walk through Columbus Park ㉑ and a bit farther along for some good dim sum ㉒. If you prefer noodles ㉓, take a left onto Bowery Doyers Street. Then take Pell Street back to Bowery, and after the entrance to the Manhattan Bridge take a left on Canal Street. Have a drink ㉔, a healthy lunch ㉕, or on Division Street a hearty bite ㉖. Turn left on Essex Street to shop at the fair ㉗. Turn left onto Grand Street and right again on Orchard Street. On Broome Street you can eat ㉘, see art ㉙, and do some shopping ㉚. Walk back and take a right onto Eldridge Street for more art ㉛. Turn right on Delancey Street and walk two blocks to turn right on Orchard Street ㉜. Turn around and head the opposite direction on Orchard, turn left on Stanton Street, then right onto Allen Street for live music ㉝. Turn back around and turn left on Stanton Street for more music ㉞ and some shopping ㉟. Take a left on Suffolk Street where there is more art to be seen ㊱. Turn back around on Suffolk and turn right on Rivington Street to score a nice vintage item ㊲.

SIGHTS & ATTRACTIONS

7 Castle Clinton was built on a man-made island and completed in 1811. Its initial purpose was to protect the harbor from the British. Later it functioned as a theater and then as a landing depot for immigrants—between 1855 and 1890, some 8 million immigrants passed through here. For a time after that, the castle was even home to the New York Aquarium. Today you can purchase tickets here for the ferry over to the Statue of Liberty and Ellis Island.
Battery Park, www.nps.gov/cacl, tel. 212-344-7220, daily 7:45am-5pm, free, 1 train to South Ferry, 4 & 5 trains to Bowling Green

8 On the site where Fort Amsterdam stood during the 17th century now stands the US Custom House. Today the first three stories of the building house the **National Museum of the American Indian.** The custom house was completed in 1907, at a time when the Port of New York was the most important port in the United States. Sixty percent of all customs duties in the country were collected here. The museum has permanent and temporary exhibitions about the Native peoples of the Americas.
1 Bowling Green, www.nmai.si.edu, tel. 212-514-3700, Mon-Wed & Fri-Sun 10am-5pm, Thu 10am-8pm, free, 4 & 5 trains to Bowling Green, 1 train to South Ferry

11 Federal Hall National Memorial stands on the site where George Washington took the oath of office as the first U.S. president and where the first Congress convened. The current building was previously a U.S. customs house and once contained more than $300 million in silver and gold. Today it is a museum about Washington's inauguration, freedom of the press, and Federal Hall (the first capitol), which stood on this spot.
26 Wall St, at Broad St, www.nps.gov/feha, tel. 212-825-6990, Mon-Fri 9am-5pm, free, 2 & 3 trains to Wall St

13 Trinity Church is a charming, beautiful, old example of Neo-Gothic architecture, which miraculously was unscathed after 9/11. Alexander Hamilton is buried in the cemetery, as well as a few of the earliest Dutch colonists.

MICHAEL CAMERON LYNCH   DAVID ROBERT ME
ENT A. CANGELOSI   JOSEPH RYAN ALLEN   LA
TIMOTHY D. BETTERLY   RICHARD H
CK LADLEY   JOHN M. POCHER   JAMES
BERNARD PIETRONICO   JOSEPH PLUMITA

75 Broadway, www.trinitywallstreet.org, tel. 212-602-0800, Mon-Fri 7am-6pm, Sat 8am-4pm, Sun 7am-4pm, Sun service 9am & 11:15am, free, 2, 3, 4 & 5 trains to Wall St, 1, N & R trains to Rector St, J, M & Z trains to Broad St

Take the time to visit the **9/11 Memorial Museum,** where—among other things—you can check out an exhibition that presents the attack on the World Trade Center in three parts: the events of the day itself, the background leading up to that day, and the impact in the period that followed. The museum also regularly organizes films and lectures.
1 Albany St, www.911memorial.org/museum, tel. 212-266-5211, Sun-Thu 9am-8pm, Fri-Sat 9am-9pm, $24, A, C, J, Z, 2, 3, 4 & 5 trains to Fulton St, E train to World Trade Center

St. Paul's Chapel has miraculously been able to survive the Revolutionary War and two terrorist attacks on the World Trade Center relatively unaltered. In the hours, weeks, and months that followed 9/11, the chapel became a place where rescue and recovery workers from Ground Zero received care and support. Visitors can see photos and read stories from this time inside the chapel.
209 Broadway, www.trinitywallstreet.org/about/stpaulschapel, tel. 212-602-0800, Mon-Sat 10am-6pm, Sun 7am-6pm, Sun service 8am, 9:15am & 8pm, free, 2, 3, 4, 5, A & C trains to Broadway-Nassau St

City Hall houses the office of the mayor, the city council, and various other offices. There is a small collection of memorabilia on display in the building and free tours are given during the week. However, you must make a reservation for tours online (public tours city hall).
Broadway, at City Hall Park, www.nyc.gov, tel. 212-639-9675, open Mon-Fri 9am-5pm, free, 4, 5 & 6 trains to Brooklyn Bridge-City Hall, R Train to City Hall

The awe-inspiring **Municipal Building** was built starting in 1909 to create additional office space for municipal agencies. The building is surmounted by the copper statue "Civic Fame," a female figure holding a five-pointed crown that symbolizes the five boroughs of the city.
1 Centre St, www.nyc.gov, Mon-Fri 9am-5:30pm, free, 4, 5 & 6 trains to Brooklyn Bridge-City Hall, R train to City Hall

FOOD & DRINK

❶ In New York, life is mainly lived indoors, but **Celestine** is a bar/restaurant with a phenomenal view of the East River and the Manhattan Bridge. They serve delicious (East) Mediterranean food, good wine, and great cocktails.
1 John St, www.celestinebk.com, tel. 718-522-5356, Mon-Fri 11:30am-10:30pm, Sat-Sun 10am-11pm, $29, F train to York St

❸ This cozy little café is famous for its cookies, and you'll want to spend time here with friends and family, sampling as many cookies as possible. **One Girl Cookies** is a true New York landmark that has been reviewed by the likes of Oprah and *New York Magazine*. They also have great coffee, cupcakes, and pie.
33 Main St, onegirlcookies.com, tel. 212-675-4996, Mon-Fri 8am-6pm, Sat-Sun 9am-6pm, cookies from $0.80, F train to York St

❾ Fraunces Tavern is more than just a bar and restaurant; it is also a museum where you can learn about the Revolutionary War. Founding Father George Washington and his officers celebrated their victory here with a festive dinner.
54 Pearl St, at Broad St, www.frauncestavern.com, tel. 212-968-1776, daily 11am-10pm (bar open late), from $24, R & 1 trains to Whitehall St/South Ferry, 2 & 3 trains to Wall St

❿ Stone Street gets its name from being the first paved road in the city. Today many restaurants fill the 19th-century buildings here, and the street has become a popular spot among those who work on Wall Street. When the weather is nice, the restaurants set up wooden tables right in the middle of the street. For delicious breakfast and coffee, head to the French bakery Financier.
Stone St, between Broad St and Hanover Street Square, 2 & 3 trains to Wall Street, R train to Whitehall St

⓬ Amid the busy rush of the stock market, money, and skyscrapers, you'll find an oasis of good food and cozy European vibes. **Schilling** is an Austrian eatery that serves home-country classics such as *spätzle* and *wiener schnitzel*. And since its owner also owns Edi & The Wolf (which has a Michelin star), you can expect excellent food.
109 Washington St, www.schillingnyc.com, tel. 212-406-1200, Mon-Fri noon-3pm & 5pm-10pm, Sat-Sun 5pm-10pm, $24, 5 train to Wall St

㉒ Who doesn't like dim sum? These steamed little dough packages with filling were originally a Chinese breakfast snack, but at **Dim Sum Go Go** you can eat them all day long. The interior is somewhat 1980s modern, but don't be fooled—the Michelin stickers are a dead giveaway that you're in for a culinary treat. And since it can get quite busy, we advise you to get there just between lunch and dinner—around 3pm to 4pm.

5 E Broadway, www.dimsumgogonyc.com, tel. 212-732-0797, daily 10am-11pm, from $5, Q train to Canal St

㉓ Noodles are as traditional in China as dim sum, but there are few places left that still make their own. At **Tasty Hand-Pulled Noodles** they make a classic dough that is stretched into long strands of fresh noodles, which will end up in your soup and other delicious dishes.

1 Doyers St, www.tastyhandpullednoodlesnyc.com, tel. 212-891-1817, daily 10:30am-10:30pm, from $9, Q train to Canal St

㉔ At the dark **Bar Belly,** you get to enjoy oysters, cocktails, and music. From Wednesday through to Sunday there is live music during happy hour; later on, a DJ takes over. In addition to oysters, they serve small bar snacks. Hungry for something more substantial? Visit Bar Belly's bigger brother, The Fat Radish.

14b Orchard St, www.barbellynyc.com, tel. 917-488-0943, Mon-Tue 5pm-1am, Wed-Thu 5pm-2pm, Fri 5pm-4am, Sat 3pm-4am, Sun 5pm-11pm, from $13, B & D trains to Grand Street, F train to East Broadway

㉕ Tucked between a variety of Chinese stores you'll find **Dimes.** This small spot is a great place to come for breakfast, lunch, or dinner. The clean, light interior will immediately put you in a good mood. The restaurant serves up wholesome, seasonal dishes, which makes it popular among the city's health conscious.

49 Canal St, www.dimesnyc.com, tel. 212-925-1300, Mon-Thu 8am-11pm, Fri 8am-midnight, Sat 9am-11pm, Sun 9am-10:30pm, from $12, F train to East Broadway, J & M trains to Essex St

㉖ The restaurant **The Fat Radish** is located in a former sausage factory at the edge of Chinatown and the Lower East Side. Some of the building's

history is still noticeable, thanks to the restaurant's industrial interior with high ceilings and brick walls. Here they serve simple, healthy dishes.
17 Orchard St, www.thefatradishnyc.com, tel. 212-300-4053, Mon-Wed 5:30pm-10pm, Thu-Fri 5:30-11pm, Sat 11am-3:30pm & 5:30pm-11pm, Sun 11am-3:30pm & 5:30pm-10pm, $23, B & D trains to Grand St, F train to East Broadway

28 The atmosphere in this charming corner restaurant is warm and inviting. **Dudley's** is always busy, and local residents often stop here for a bite on their way to or from work. Have a cocktail at the bar or sit at the window for some good people watching. The classic American fare they serve here is simple but delicious. Try, for example, the Bronte Burger.
85 Orchard St, www.dudleysnyc.com, tel. 212-925-7355, daily 9am-1am, $20, B & D trains to Grand St, F train to Delancey St

SHOPPING

2 **Usagi** is actually several shops in one. With an art gallery, bookstore, and coffee bar, it is a true concept store. *Usagi*, which means "rabbit" in Japanese, symbolizes spring and renewal. The shop is the perfect spot to recharge from the hustle and bustle of this crazy city.
163 Plymouth St, www.usaginy.com, tel. 718-801-8037, Mon-Fri 8:30am-6pm, Sat 11am-6pm, F train to York St

15 **Century 21** is where bargain hunters' dreams come true. At this department store you'll find racks of brand-name, designer clothes at significantly discounted prices. The store is so big, it may take a while before you even make it to the department you initially came in for.
21 Dey St, www.c21stores.com, tel. 212-227-9092, Mon-Wed 7:45am-9pm, Thu-Fri 7:45am-9:30pm, Sat 10am-9pm, Sun 11am-8pm, N & R trains to Cortlandt St, 4 & 5 trains to Fulton St, E train to World Trade Center

㉒ CityStore is New York's official souvenir shop. Here you can buy tiles from the city's subway stations, genuine taxicab medallions, and official merchandise from the NYPD and the NYFD.

1 Centre St, North Plaza, www.nyc.gov/citystore, tel. 212-386-0007, Mon-Fri 10am-5pm, 4, 5, 6, J & M trains to Brooklyn Bridge, 1, 2, A, C & E trains to Chambers St, R train to City Hall

㉗ For beautiful antiques, vintage items, and a variety of other trinkets head to **Hester Street Fair.** Here you'll also find lots of food vendors, many of whom offer samples. This small market always attracts big crowds.

Corner of Hester and Essex streets, www.hesterstreetfair.com, late April-late Oct Sat 11am-6pm, F train to E Broadway or Delancey St, F, J, M & Z trains to Essex St

㉚ The minimalist store **Top Hat** offers a mix of design stationery items and other related products: notebooks, stamps, leather pencil cases, and bags. In addition, the store sells unique home decor and lifestyle products.

245 Broome St, www.tophatnyc.com, tel. 212-677-4240, Tue-Sat noon-8pm, Sun 11am-7pm, F train to Delancey St, J, M & Z trains to Essex St

㉟ For a long time, this location was home to the hip concept store Pixiemarket. Now, however, the owners run the shop **Frankie Shop**—Pixiemarket's big sister. It is geared toward the fashion-conscious woman with unique taste who likes to be well dressed for every occasion. Frankie offers a changing collection of London- and Scandinavia-style clothes and accessories—including shoes, jewelry, and bags—from independent designers with a distinct, edgy look.

100 Stanton St, www.thefrankieshop.com, tel. 212-253-0953, Mon-Sat noon-8pm, Sun noon-7pm, F train to 2nd Av

㊲ Edith Machinist is an enormous vintage store full of shoes and bags from both well-known and unknown brands. Prices may be on the high side, but rest assured you are getting something unique and exclusive. See something in the store you're sorry you passed up? Don't sweat it; you can continue shopping online.

104 Rivington St, www.edithmachinist.com, tel. 212-979-9992, Mon, Fri, Sun noon-6pm, Tue-Thu & Sat noon-7pm, F train to Delancey St, J, M & Z trains to Essex St

MORE TO EXPLORE

④ Jane's Carousel dates back to 1922. For years it operated in Youngstown, Ohio. The developer of the park where it currently stands bought it in 1983, together with his wife, Jane. After years of renovation it was restored to its original glory, and Jane's Carousel reopened in 2011. Now young and old can enjoy a ride for a fair price.

Old Dock St, www.janescarousel.org, tel. 718-222-2502, Sep-May Thu-Sun 11am-6pm, May-Sep Wed-Mon 11am-7pm, $2, F train to York St

⑤ If you want to go from Brooklyn to Manhattan, the **East River Ferry** is one of the best alternatives to the subway. A ticket costs about the same as a subway fare, and it takes you from Dumbo Pier 1 to the Wall Street stop at the end of Manhattan in a mere 4 minutes. You can also take a ferry to 34th Street (Herald Square) or even to Coney Island (the beach with an amusement park).

Furman St & Old Fulton St, www.eastriverferry.com/brooklynbridgepark-dumbo, tel. 844-469-3377, daily 6:30am-9:30pm, $2.75, F train to York St

⑥ A ride on the **Staten Island Ferry** is a fun and free way to see the Statue of Liberty and the New York City skyline. Aside from the occasional savvy tourist, the ferry is primarily used by commuters from Staten Island. All told, a trip to Staten Island and back takes about an hour, and you never have to wait too long for the next boat.

Whitehall Terminal, 4 Whitehall St, www.siferry.com, tel. 718-815-2628, 24 hours a day, 7 days a week, free, 1 train to South Ferry, 4 & 5 trains to Bowling Green, N & R trains to Whitehall St

⑱ Construction of the 5,989-foot-long (1,825 m) **Brooklyn Bridge** began in 1870 and was completed 13 years later. The Gothic granite towers and steel cables are now an iconic New York City landmark. Walk out across the bridge for an amazing view of both Manhattan and Brooklyn, which is particularly beautiful at sunset.

Park Row, near Centre Street, 4, 5 & 6 trains to Brooklyn Bridge-City Hall, N & R trains to City Hall

㉑ Columbus Park is located in what was once one of the worst neighborhoods in the city. Today, however, the park is the peaceful backdrop to scenes of women chatting over games of cards, men hunkering over Chinese checkerboards, and children playing and having fun. There is always lots of activity here.

Mulberry St, between Bayard St and Worth St, www.nycgovparks.org, daily, A, C, E, J, M, N, Q, R, Z & 6 trains to Canal St

㉙ The contemporary art on display at **Catinca Tabacaru Gallery** changes from month to month. The gallery features conceptual works by young artists from both the United States and abroad. Several times a year they publish catalogs about upcoming art fairs and cultural projects to keep an eye out for.

250 Broome St, catincatabacaru.com, tel. 603-957-1354, Wed-Sun 11am-6pm, F train to Delancey St, J, M & Z trains to Essex St

③ **YUI Gallery** is an art gallery owned by Yuchen Wang and Qiaoyi Shi. They specialize in abstract, modern, and pop art from young and upcoming artists. It's also a quiet oasis in the hustle and bustle of Chinatown.

131 Eldridge St, www.yui.nyc, tel. 518-520-0888, Sat-Sun noon-5pm, J & Z trains to Bowery

㉜ Discover what life was like for millions of New York immigrants in the late 19th and early 20th centuries at the **Lower East Side Tenement Museum.** To visit the museum, you must sign up for a tour, and making reservations beforehand is recommended.

103 Orchard St, www.tenement.org, tel. 877-975-3786, daily 10am-6:30pm, Thu 10am-8:30pm, $25, F, J, M & Z trains to Delancey St/Essex St

㉝ **Rockwood Music Hall** is a bar and a pop stage where every New York musician has played at least once—or is intending to do so. The complex consists of three halls, each with a different feel: casual, intimate, or concertlike. In most rooms a different artist plays every hour until midnight— and all in various styles, so there's something for everyone to enjoy! Check their website or pop by to see the schedule.

196 Allen St, www.rockwoodmusichall.com, tel. 212-477-4115, see website for times, F train to 2nd Av, M-15 bus to Allen St/Stanton St

㉞ **Arlene's Grocery** is a firm fixture in the New York music scene. Famous musicians and bands, such as Arcade Fire, Lana del Rey, and of course Jeff Buckley, have played at this establishment. Every night there's a great band or act, always from a different genre. Admission is fair as well.

95 Stanton St, www.arlenesgrocery.net, tel. 212-358-1633, Mon-Thu 4pm-4am, Fri-Sun 3pm-4am, $10, F train to 2nd Av

㊱ Many talented young artists selected from around the world hold their first solo exhibitions at **Rachel Uffner.** The primarily abstract art is displayed in an amazingly light space.

170 Suffolk St, www.racheluffnergallery.com, tel. 212-274-0064, Wed-Sun 10am-6pm, F train to Delancey St, M train to 2nd Av, J, M & Z trains to Essex St

NOLITA, SOHO, WEST VILLAGE & HIGH LINE

ABOUT THE WALK

On this walk you'll see several charming New York City neighborhoods. Discover the designer boutiques and popular restaurants in the NoLIta and SoHo neighborhoods, and enjoy the treelined streets and beautiful 18th- and 19th-century architecture in the romantic West Village. West Village is situated on the banks of the Hudson River, so as you walk or cycle through this neighborhood, you'll probably enjoy a wonderful breeze.

THE NEIGHBORHOODS

There's a stark difference between neighborhoods south of 14th Street and their more Uptown counterparts. The small, trendy **NoLIta** (short for "North of Little Italy") is a small, square-shaped area located between East Houston, the Bowery, Broome Street, and Lafayette. Elizabeth Street in particular is well known for its beautiful shops and boutiques.

SoHo (short for "South of Houston" Street) was originally an industrial area full of factories and warehouses. Today, however, this hip neighborhood is a major trendsetter in the fashion world. With its grand, cast-iron warehouses, luxury boutiques, fashion houses, and art galleries, SoHo offers some of the best shopping in the city.

The **West Village,** which is part of Greenwich Village, is also known as "Little Bohemia." It is home to many famous people and accommodates their creative lifestyles. At the northwest corner of Greenwich Village lies the **Meatpacking District.** This used to be a shadier part of the city but today is filled with trendy stores and popular restaurants that line the old cobblestone streets, and is a great place for going out.

Since opening in 2009, the **High Line** Park has been incredibly popular. It is located on an old train line spur that runs through Chelsea and the Meatpacking

District dozens of feet above street level. Until 1980, the train line was used to bring goods to and from the area's warehouses. After falling into disuse, the line was slated for demolition until local residents came up with the idea of creating an elevated park. Since most of the buildings in the surrounding area are relatively low, the High Line offers an amazing view out over the Hudson River and Chelsea neighborhood.

SHORT ON TIME? HERE ARE THE HIGHLIGHTS:

2 TACOMBI + **11** MCNALLY JACKSON BOOKS + **21** GREENWICH LETTERPRESS + **33** THE HIGH LINE + **34** CHELSEA MARKET

TIPS

// A must-do walk if it's your first time in the Big Apple
// This route leads you through authentic New York City neighborhoods
// Take an evening stroll along the Hudson River

NOLITA, SOHO, WEST VILLAGE & HIGH LINE

LEGEND

- >> SIGHTS & ATTRACTIONS
- >> FOOD & DRINK
- >> SHOPPING
- >> MORE TO EXPLORE
- >> WALK HIGHLIGHT

WALK DESCRIPTION 2 (approx. 5.6 mi/9 km)

Start with a cup of tea ❶ and breakfast or remember this place for tacos later in the day ❷. Continue onto E Houston for the mural ❸. Walk back to go shopping ❹ and turn left for the New Museum ❺ and over Bowery to Delancey for a croissant ❻. Walk to the Bowery and take a left for pizza ❼. Turn around and take a right on Elizabeth Street for a vegan lunch ❽ or continue straight, take a right onto Broome Street, and then left onto Mulberry Street for the Italian American Museum ❾. Turn right on Grand Street and right again for good wine ❿. Walk until you get to Prince Street: take a right for a bookshop ⓫. Turn left, then right on Crosby Street until you get to Grand Street where you can go shopping ⓬. Turn right onto Grand Street and right again to Broome for yarn and needles ⓭. Take a left onto Broadway for some sightseeing ⓮. Go left and right again on Mercer Street ⓯. Walk back to Spring Street and take Greene Street to the left ⓰. Go right and follow Broome Street until Varvick. Here you take a right and continue onto West Houston to catch a movie ⓱. Take a left onto 6th Ave and go left on Bleecker Street for a cheese board ⓲. Take a left onto Morton Street, 7th Avenue, and Bedford Street, and left again on Carmine Street for coffee ⓳. Walk along, over 6th Avenue and take a left on West 4th Street until Christopher Park ⓴. There, you can buy nice cards ㉑. Take a left on Greenwich Avenue and feel the Tuscan vibe on 10th Street ㉒. Make another immediate left on 10th Street and walk toward the West Village. Turn left on 4th Street, right onto Christopher Street, and right onto Bleecker Street ㉓. Take a right onto 10th where you can have a drink on the right ㉔. For a fish burger ㉕ take a left onto 4th street. Take a left on Perry to see where they filmed *Sex and the City* ㉖. Walk along 4th Street and take a left onto 11th for a special bookshop ㉗, take a left and left again for a glass of wine ㉘, and left again onto Bleecker Street for cupcakes ㉙. Walk until you get to Horatio Street and take a left. Turn right on Washington for American art ㉚. Walk on, enjoy the Biergarten ㉛ or a rooftop bar ㉜. Walk on the High Line ㉝ and finish things off with a visit to the Chelsea Market ㉞.

SIGHTS & ATTRACTIONS

❸ The **Bowery Mural** is actually an open-air canvas—a wall where both well-known and less well-known artists display their art. It's an initiative from Tony Goldman, Jeffrey Deitch, and Deitch Projects that are responsible for the real estate of which the mural is a part. The first artist was Keith Haring, who added a piece on the wall in 1970 and started almost 50 years of Urban Graffiti Art in the neighborhood.

76 E Houston St, B, D, F & M trains to Broadway-Lafayette

❺ Visit the **New Museum** to see international exhibitions of contemporary art, featuring new art and new ideas. Emerging artists are given a platform for their work here, which often leads to exciting and adventurous works, including everything from sound installations to a simulated spaceship interior. In 2007 the museum moved to a bigger home on Bowery, where you can easily spend hours taking in all the artwork.

235 Bowery, www.newmuseum.org, tel. 212-219-1222, Wed & Fri-Sun 11am-6pm, Thu 11am-9pm, $16, J & Z trains to Bowery, F train to 2nd Av

❾ This small museum in Little Italy began in 1999 as a temporary exhibit. It was met with overwhelming success, which led to the opening of the **Italian American Museum** in 2001. Here you can learn all about the history of Italian Americans and see a variety of cultural exhibits.

155 Mulberry St, www.italianamericanmuseum.org, tel. 212-965-9000, Fri-Sun noon-6pm, Mon-Thu open to groups by appt only, minimum donation $5, J, N, Q, Z & 6 trains to Canal St

❿ The **Singer Building** is an excellent place to start if you're looking to explore SoHo's cast-iron architecture. The building was erected in 1902 by the Singer Manufacturing Company, known primarily for sewing machines. Today the building houses numerous offices and apartments.

561 Broadway, between Prince and Spring streets, not open to the public, N & R trains to Prince St, 6 train to Spring St, B, D, F & M trains to Broadway-Lafayette

15 The small, unassuming house at **105 Mercer Street** has a rather remarkable history. One year after it was built in 1831, it became one of SoHo's most thriving brothels. It's hard to imagine that, back in the day, SoHo was once the city's red-light district.

105 Mercer St, between Prince and Spring streets, not open to the public, N & R trains to Prince St, 6 train to Spring St, B, D, F & M trains to Broadway-Lafayette

16 You'll find some of SoHo's most beautiful cast-iron buildings on **Greene Street.** The building at numbers 72-76, known as the "King of Greene Street," is one of the prime examples of this type of architecture in the neighborhood. Take a step back to fully admire the tall windows and Corinthian columns.

72-76 Greene St, between Spring and Broome streets, C, E & 6 trains to Spring St, B, D, F & M trains to Broadway-Lafayette

26 For years the **townhouse** at 66 Perry Street was the backdrop for the series *Sex and the City*. The show's main character, **Carrie Bradshaw,** lived here in the West Village, and since then this quaint street has seen a rise in popularity. Every day, countless fans come here to pose for a photo in front of the charming brownstone. It's nice—for fans of the show, at any rate—to check out the street and see where this legendary sitcom took place.

66 Perry St, 1 train to Christopher Street-Sheridan Square

30 The **Whitney Museum of American Art** is a collection of America's most diverse forms of artistic expression from the 20th and 21st centuries. See works from Jasper Johns and Andy Warhol, along with everything from paintings and sculptures to videos and performance art. The Whitney Biennial, which spotlights young, unknown talents, is particularly well known. The museum was established in 1931 by the wealthy sculptor and art collector Gertrude Vanderbilt Whitney with 700 works from her own collection. Today the permanent collection includes around 18,000 pieces of art. Architect Renzo Piano designed the new Whitney building, which opened in early 2015.

99 Gansevoort St, www.whitney.org, tel. 212-570-3600, Mon, Wed & Sun 10:30am-6pm, Thu-Sat 10:30am-10pm, $22, A, C & E trains to 14th St, L train to 8th Av

FOOD & DRINK

❶ If you are a true tea enthusiast, then **T Shop** is your spot. This is the destination for everyone who is crazy about tea, and especially if you think of yourself as a bit of a tea connoisseur. At T Shop you can buy tea as well as drink it. You can try a tasting or opt for a *Gong Fu tea service*: a specialized tea ceremony for you and your friends.

247 Elizabeth St, www.tshopny.com, daily noon-9pm, cup of tea $5, tea ceremony $80, R & W trains to Prince St

❷ The upbeat atmosphere and delicious food at this Mexican taqueria make **Tacombi** a favorite among New Yorkers. Here they serve up authentic tacos, fresher-than-fresh salsa, and fruity drinks right out of an old Volkswagen bus. Tip: the hearty huevos make for a great weekend breakfast.

267 Elizabeth St, www.tacombi.com, tel. 917-727-0179, Sun-Wed 11am-midnight, Thu-Sat 11am-1am, Sat-Sun breakfast starts at 10am, from $11, B, D, F & M trains to Broadway-Lafayette

❻ In this café, you'll experience a little bit of Paris in New York: it's one of the best in the city and certainly not a chain. **Ceci-Cela Patisserie** also has a phenomenal lunch menu.

14 Delancey St, www.cecicelanyc.com, tel. 212-274-9179, Mon-Fri 6:30am-8pm, Sat 7am-9pm, Sun 7am-8pm, from $7, J & Z trains to Bowery

❼ **Lombardi's** is a New York treasure that has been turning pizza into high art since 1905. Families sit at casual tables covered in red-and-white checked tablecloths, and pizzas emerge from the coal oven with sooty crusts and wads of fresh mozzarella. At the bar, you can wait with a Peroni.

32 Spring St, www.firstpizza.com, tel. 212-941-7994, Sun-Thu 11:30am-11pm, Fri-Sat 11:30am-midnight, pizzas from $20, J & Z trains to Bowery

❽ Come to the juice bar and café **The Butcher's Daughter** for a yummy breakfast or healthy lunch and a fresh juice or smoothie. Despite what the name might suggest, don't expect to find any giant slabs of meat here. According to the restaurant, they treat fruits and vegetables as a butcher would treat meat. The

Lenana, Kenya '22
Brazil, Daterra Farm '16
Malabapa, El Salvador '21
Prodigy espresso '15
Prodigy decaf '16

OREO SANDWICH

restaurant's interior has a rugged, industrial look but with a fresh, feminine twist. In the summertime, they also set up long picnic tables outside.

19 Kenmare St, www.thebutchersdaughter.com, tel. 212-219-3434, daily 8am-10pm, from $11, J & Z trains to Bowery

⑩ La Compagnie des Vins Surnaturels is one of the best wine bars in the city. The ambience is amazing, the interior is relaxed, and the bar snacks are outstanding. The owners have worked at Eleven Madison Park—an award-winning, Michelin-starred restaurant—so quality is guaranteed!

249 Centre St, www.compagnienyc.com, tel. 212-343-3660, Mon-Fri 5pm-2am, Sat-Sun 3pm-2am, wine from $15, 6 train to Spring St

⑱ The owners of the adjacent **Murray's Cheese Bar** must have had so many people come in for a taste that they came up with the special concept of Murray's Cheese Bar. Now everyone gets to enjoy all of Murray's cheeses, including snacks, hams, and even dinner with a great glass of wine. If you can't choose, the waiters love to help you create tastings and pairings that are always a match made in heaven.

264 Bleecker St, www.murrayscheesebar.com, tel. 646-476-8882, Mon-Tue 4pm-10pm, Wed-Thu 4pm-midnight, Fri noon-midnight, Sat 11am-midnight, Sun 11am-10pm, from $13, 1 train to Christopher St

⑲ Good, fair-trade coffee is the philosophy at **Prodigy Coffee,** and the beans are freshly roasted in nearby Brooklyn. In addition to coffee, this intimate café with just a few tables also offers a selection of yummy pastries.

33 Carmine St, www.prodigycoffee.com, tel. 212-414-4142, Mon-Fri 7am-7pm, Sat-Sun 8am-7pm, from $2.50, A, B, C, D, E & F trains to West 4th St

㉒ Rosemary's is an Italian trattoria with a perfect vibe. It is one of those places you look at and think, yes, that's where we'll sit down! It's inspired by the owner's grandmother, and Rosemary's is an Italian restaurant that grows its own vegetables on the rooftop garden and has a firm link to Tuscany.

18 Greenwich Ave, www.rosemarysnyc.com, tel. 212-647-1818, Mon-Thu 8am-11pm, Fri 8am-midnight, Sat 10am-midnight, Sun 10am-11pm, from $14, 1 train to Christopher St

24 The casual West Village bar **Wilfie & Nell** is always a happening place in the evenings after work and on the weekends until late night. People come here for a drink and a chat with those around them, whether it be tourists or locals. Typically, there is only room to stand, although there are some stools at the bar.
228 W 4th St, www.wilfieandnell.com, tel. 212-242-2990, Mon-Wed 4pm-3am, Thu-Fri 4pm-4am, Sat-Sun noon-4am, from $9, 1 & 2 trains to Christopher St, A, B, C, D, E, F & M trains to W 4th St

25 As soon as you walk in the door at **Mary's Fish Camp,** you'll feel as if you're somewhere on the water thanks to the crisp, blue interior and the smell of fresh fish. The restaurant has an extensive fish menu, and on Mondays you can get a nice bottle of wine with your meal for just $20—a great price by NYC standards.
64 Charles St, www.marysfishcamp.com, tel. 646-486-2185, Mon-Sat noon-3pm & 6pm-11pm, Sun noon-4pm, from $22, 1 & 2 trains to Christopher St, A, B, C, D, E, F & M trains to W 4th St

28 **Aria Wine Bar** serves high-quality Italian food. The open bar, along with the rustic wooden tables, white tiles, and untreated brick walls make for a laid-back atmosphere. The restaurant is always busy, so be sure to get here early.
117 Perry St, www.ariawinebar.com, tel. 212-242-4233, Sun-Thu 11am-10:30pm, Fri-Sat 11am-11pm, pasta from $12, 1 train to Christopher St, 1, 2 & 3 trains to 14th St

31 Tucked away under the High Line you'll find the **Biergarten.** Come here to play an old-fashioned game of Ping Pong. The Biergarten draws a mix of neighborhood locals, tourists, and New York City professionals. Be sure to bring along your ID.
848 Washington St, www.standardhotels.com, tel. 212-645-4100, Mon-Wed & Sun noon-1am, Thu-Sat noon-2am, from $8, A, C & E trains to 14th St, L train to 8th Av

32 **Le Bain** is a trendy rooftop bar. During the week, it is fairly easy to get in. On the weekend it can get really busy, but put on your finest threads and try your luck. Who knows, maybe you'll bump into someone famous.
848 Washington St, in the Standard Hotel, www.standardhotels.com, tel. 212-645-4646, Mon 4pm-midnight, Tue-Thu 4pm-4am, Fri-Sat 2pm-4am, Sun 2pm-3am, from $12, A, C & E trains to 14th St, L train to 8th Av

🌟 Oreo cookies were once made in this old factory building. Today **Chelsea Market** is a place to come for good food and shopping. There are many food options available here, but the lobster roll at Lobster Place is highly recommended. Look for a place to sit in the hall and enjoy people-watching as you eat. If there are no free tables, take your food outside and head upstairs to the High Line.

75 9th Ave, www.chelseamarket.com, Mon-Sat 7am-9pm, Sun 8am-8pm, A, C & E trains to 14th St

SHOPPING

④ The perfume store **Le Labo** is a true fragrance laboratory, complete with old workbenches, bottle-lined shelves, and vintage cases. Let them create a unique fragrance for you here on the spot from a mix of natural ingredients. To make it extra special, you can even have the bottle monogrammed. Le Labo also sells its New York City Exclusive—a true NYC fragrance.

233 Elizabeth St, www.lelabofragrances.com, tel. 212-219-2230, daily 11am-7pm, F train to 2nd Av, J train to Bowery

🌟 With just two floors, **McNally Jackson Books** is far from the largest bookstore in New York. However, it does have one of the best selections, and the store aspires "to be the center of Manhattan's literary culture." Grab a seat on a comfortable sofa and thumb through a good book or magazine. The store also has a café that sells good coffee, sandwiches, and quiches.

52 Prince St, www.mcnallyjackson.com, tel. 212-274-1160, Mon-Sat 10am-10pm, Sun 10am-9pm, B, D, F & M trains to Broadway-Lafayette, N & R trains to Prince St

⑫ You might not expect to come across a surf shop in New York City, but that is exactly what you'll find here. **Saturdays Surf** is all about a unique combination of surf supplies, art, books, clothing, accessories, and a good espresso bar. Enjoy your coffee and a moment of calm on the terrace out back.

31 Crosby St, www.saturdaysnyc.com, tel. 212-966-7875, Mon-Sun 10am-7pm, J, N, Q, Z & 6 trains to Canal St, 6 train to Spring St

⑬ Arts and crafts are totally back, right?! At **Purl SoHo** there is a huge selection of specialty yarn, wool, knitting materials, and needles. They also give outstanding advice and (free) patterns, and they organize lessons and other fun events. Keep an eye on their website for the schedule.
459 Broome St, www.purlsoho.com, tel. 212-420-8796, Mon-Fri noon-7pm, Sat-Sun noon-6pm, N, Q, R & W trains to Canal St

㉑ Whatever occasion you are shopping for, **Greenwich Letterpress** probably has something for you. The old-school store full of cards and stationery of all sorts is exponentially nicer than your average store's card section. Nearly all of the cards are designed and printed in-house using a letterpress—a classic relief printing technique that is currently making a comeback.
15 Christopher St, www.greenwichletterpress.com, tel. 212-989-7464, Tue-Sat 11am-7pm, Sun-Mon noon-6pm, 1 train to Christopher St

㉓ Upscale hotels in Asia have been using **Aesop** products for some time. The excellent skin and hair care products are plant-based and not only smell amazing, but they are also nicely packaged. Each store has a unique interior adapted to suit the neighborhood where it is located; however, the underlying design is always recognizable: pure and stylish with earthy colors.
341 Bleecker St, www.aesop.com, tel. 347-834-5403, Mon-Wed & Sun 11am-7pm, Thu-Sat 11am-8pm, 1, 2, 3, A, B, D, E, F & M trains to Christopher St

㉗ We all know Marc Jacobs is a fashion designer, but that didn't stop him from opening a bookshop in 2010—just so he could celebrate his love of books. At **Bookmarc** they sell coffee table books and other gems in a selection curated by Marc Jacobs himself. And Bookmarc NYC is the place to be for book presentations. Richard Hell, Grace Coddington, and Anjelica Huston all held their book launches here.
400 Bleecker St, www.marcjacobs.com/bookmarc, tel. 212-620-4021, Mon-Sat 11am-7pm, Sun noon-6pm, 1 train to Christopher St

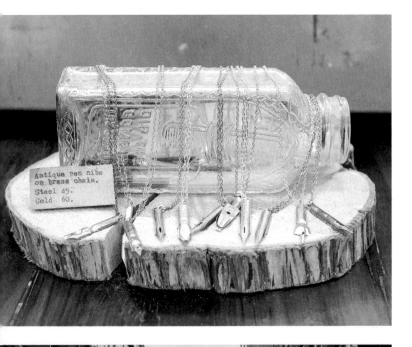

Antique pen nibs
on brass chain.
Steel 45.
Gold 60.

㉙ You'll know you're close to **Magnolia Bakery** when you begin to see people passing by carrying white boxes. Inside are the delicious cupcakes made famous by the TV series *Sex and the City*. If you're not in the mood for a cupcake, try the banana pudding.

401 Bleecker St, www.magnoliabakery.com, tel. 212-462-2572, Mon-Thu 9am-11:30pm, Fri-Sat 9am-12:30am, Sun 9am-11:30pm, from $3.25, A, C, E & L trains to 14th St, 1 train to Christopher St

MORE TO EXPLORE

⑰ From Fellini to Fassbinder, **Film Forum** has it all. This is one of the best places in New York City to come to for foreign films and documentaries.

209 W Houston St, near Varick St, www.filmforum.org, tel. 212-727-8110, daily 12:30pm-11:30pm, $13, 1 train to Houston St

⑳ In June of 1969, a violent clash at the Stonewall Inn near **Christopher Park** led to the start of the fight for equal rights for gays and lesbians. Since then, the park and its surrounding area have been the symbol of gay liberation. The park is a nice place to sit and relax. In the vicinity, especially on Christopher Street, there are a variety of LGBTQ bars and shops.

7th Ave and Christopher St, 1 train to Christopher St-Sheridan Sq

㉝ A trip to the **High Line,** an elevated park built on a former train viaduct, feels like walking on a very long balcony that extends all the way through the city. The park is 30 feet above street level and stretches 1.45 miles (2.33 km) from Gansevoort Street to West 34th Street. From up here you can look out over the Hudson River, old warehouses, and the streets of Manhattan.

Gansevoort Street to 34th Street, between 10th and 11th avenues, www.thehighline.org, daily Dec-Mar 7am-7pm, Apr-May & Oct-Nov 7am-10pm, June-Sept 7am-11pm, free, A, C, E & L trains to 8th Av/14th St

TIMES SQUARE & UNION SQUARE

ABOUT THE WALK

This walk emphasizes art and culture. You'll see MoMA and the Museum of Arts and Design, as well as the unique architecture of Grand Central Terminal. For those who love shopping, there is the upscale 5th Avenue. Be aware that it can get very busy around Times Square, with its (musical) theaters and popular retail stores. It is somewhat calmer on weekdays, except at lunchtime.

THE NEIGHBORHOODS

New York is known around the world for **Times Square,** where yellow cabs cruise past giant screens and neon lights, and for the **Empire State Building,** with its breathtaking views of the city. It's also famous for the **Flatiron Building,** the **Museum of Modern Art (MoMA),** the shopping on **5th Avenue,** and **Radio City Music Hall,** among many other things.

For more than 100 years, people have flocked to Times Square and the surrounding area for entertainment—everything from opera and vaudeville to comedy and musicals. Since the 1980s the area has undergone a process of Disneyfication. Large companies have bought up much of the area's real estate and created an inviting atmosphere for musical theaters and entertainment venues, which flourished and attracted a different crowd. **Broadway,** renowned for its theaters, cuts right through Times Square. Head to Broadway to catch shows such as *Mathilda*, *The Lion King*, *Fiddler on the Roof*, and *Rock of Ages*. Discounted tickets are available for many shows.

Shopping is the main attraction for most visitors on **5th Avenue.** Between 60th Street and 34th Street, you'll find countless upscale stores as well as large flagship stores from brands such as Apple and Abercrombie & Fitch.

To the south lies **Gramercy Park,** the only park in New York City that is accessible only to local residents. At **Union Square** nearby, uptown and downtown come together in a spot where there is always something to do. Play a game of chess with a stranger or admire the work of local artists. There are plenty of great bars and restaurants here as well as the **Greenmarket** farmers market.

SHORT ON TIME? HERE ARE THE HIGHLIGHTS:

5 MOMA + 9 ROCKEFELLER CENTER + 14 BRYANT PARK + 15 NEW YORK PUBLIC LIBRARY + 30 ABC CARPET & HOME/ABC KITCHEN

TIPS

// A must-do walk if it's your first time in the Big Apple
// Allow yourself plenty of time to visit museums
// Visit the Empire State Building extra early or really late at night

TIMES SQUARE & UNION SQUARE

LEGEND

>> SIGHTS & ATTRACTION
>> FOOD & DRINK
>> SHOPPING
>> MORE TO EXPLORE
>> WALK HIGHLIGHT

0   0.25
0   0.25 km

Subway Line ⌐ Ⓜ *Times Square*
       A-C-E   ⌐Station Nam

© MOO

WALK 3 DESCRIPTION (approx. 7.8 mi/12.5 km)

Begin the walk at the Museum of Arts and Design ❶. Then walk to the right and turn right on 7th Avenue. Turn left on 56th Street for a good burger ❷. Go left on 6th Avenue, then right on Central Park South. At the corner of 5th Avenue you'll see a historic hotel ❸. Turn down 5th Avenue and check out the window displays. On 55th Street take a left, then left on Park Avenue, and right on 56th Street. Go right on Lexington Avenue and grab a sandwich and espresso ❹. Turn right on 53rd Street for art ❺. Walk between the buildings across from MoMA and come out at 52nd Street. Turn left here to learn about TV and radio ❻. Next door you'll find an old speakeasy ❼. Continue walking to 5th Avenue and then go right to visit a church ❽. Between 50th and 49th streets, turn right and walk down the shopping promenade. You'll see Rockefeller Center towering in front of you ❾. Continue on 50th Street to shop ❿ and for an art deco theater ⓫. On 6th Avenue turn left, then right on 47th Street toward the bustling center of NYC ⓬. Turn left on 7th Avenue and then left on 43rd Street. Photography fans will want to make a detour on 6th Avenue ⓭, then go back down the street and turn left on 42nd Street to visit the park and see some historical buildings ⓮ ⓯ ⓰. Head up the stairs at the west side of Grand Central Terminal for a cocktail ⓱. Exit the station on Lexington Avenue and be sure to look up ⓲. Head back to Park Avenue, turn left, and continue to 36th Street. Turn right here to visit a museum ⓳. Take another left on 5th Avenue, where an amazing view of the city awaits ⓴. Turn left on 32nd Street for Korean food ㉑. Continue down 5th Avenue and turn left on 30th Street, and you'll find Dover Street Market ㉒. Head back and continue to Broadway. Take a left and left again to 28th Street for lunch ㉓. Turn right to get back to 5th Avenue for cocktails at a rooftop bar ㉔. Turn right for vintage designer clothing on 25th Street ㉕. Continue on through Madison Square Park, have a lime rickey on 5th Avenue ㉖ and view the old skyscraper ㉗. Go left and right down Broadway and turn left on 20th Street to take in some history ㉘. Go back to Broadway for some shopping ㉙ ㉚. Turn left on Park Avenue, then right on Gramercy Park ㉛. Make a right on Irving Place and continue to 16th Street. Then turn right to Union Square ㉜ ㉝ and end with shopping on 13th Street ㉞.

SIGHTS & ATTRACTIONS

① The **Museum of Arts and Design** (MAD) has some 2,000 items in the permanent collection alone, including objects of fashion, design, and jewelry. MAD is also known for its radical building renovation that was not very well received in the architecture world. Particularly controversial were the windows, which appear to spell out the word "hi." On the flip side, diners in the ninth-floor restaurant have an excellent view of Central Park.

2 Columbus Circle, www.madmuseum.org, tel. 212-299-7777, Tue-Wed & Sat-Sun 10am-6pm, Thu-Fri 10am-9pm, $16, 1, A, B, C & D trains to Columbus Circle

③ Many famous people have stayed at the **Plaza Hotel.** Architect Frank Lloyd Wright, for example, stayed here while designing the Guggenheim. Rooms on the north side of the hotel have a great view of Central Park. If you're not dressed too shabbily you can probably steal a peek into the lobby. Around the corner from the hotel you'll find the entrance to the luxury Plaza Food Hall, which is a genuine feast for the eyes.

768 5th Ave, www.theplaza.com, lobby open to public, N, Q & R trains to Lexington Av-59 St, 4, 5 & 6 trains to 59 St

⑤ The world-famous **Museum of Modern Art** (MoMA) has an extensive and unique collection of contemporary and modern art. There is plenty to see here, from a helicopter suspended from the ceiling and a collection of old computers to artwork by Picasso and modern video art. Don't forget to also visit the **MoMA Design Store.**

11 W 53rd St, between 5th and 6th avenues, www.moma.org, Sat-Mon & Tue-Thu 10:30am-5:30pm, Fri 10:30am-8pm, $25, E & M trains to 5 Av/53 St, B, D & E trains to 7 Av

⑥ Learn all about the history of radio and television at the **Paley Center for Media.** Watch and hear a Frank Sinatra concert, re-experience the first *Star Trek* episode, or enjoy a documentary.

25 W 52nd St, between 5th and 6th avenues, www.paleycenter.org, tel. 212-621-6600, Thu noon-8pm, Wed & Fri-Sun noon-6pm, $10, E & M trains to 5 Av/53 St, B, D, F & M trains to 47-50 Sts-Rockefeller Ctr

⑧ The impressive **St. Patrick's Cathedral** built in 1879 is the largest Gothic cathedral in the United States and can seat more than 2,000 people. Be sure to check out the Tiffany altars, the stained-glass windows, and the Pieta—the statue of Mary holding the body of Jesus.
5th Avenue, between 50th and 51st streets, www.saintpatrickscathedral.org, tel. 212-753-2261, daily 6:30am-8:45pm, free, E & M trains to 5 Av/53 St, B, D, F & M trains to 47-50 Sts-Rockefeller Ctr

⑨ In 1928 John D. Rockefeller bought a piece of property that he developed to include office buildings and public promenades. He called it **Rockefeller Center.** Come here in the winter to go ice skating next to the giant Christmas tree. You also won't want to pass up a trip to 30 Rockefeller Plaza and the observation deck, Top of the Rock, where you have an unobstructed view of Central Park and the Empire State Building.
45 Rockefeller Plaza, www.rockefellercenter.com, daily 7am-midnight, $30, E & M trains to 5 Av/53 St, B, D, F & M trains to 47-50 Sts-Rockefeller Ctr

⑫ With its bright lights, enormous billboards, and constant crowds, **Times Square** is the pulse of New York City. Under the red stairs you'll find the **TKTS Booth** where you can buy discounted tickets for shows on and off Broadway, and for dance and music performances. Sometimes you can get up to 50 percent off. Go early because the lines can be long.
Broadway and 7th Avenue, between 42nd and 47th streets, for show tickets www. tdf.org, Mon & Fri 3pm-8pm, Tue 2pm-8pm, Wed-Thu & Sat 10am-8pm, Sun 11am-7pm, N, Q, R, S, 1, 2, 3 & 7 trains to Times Sq-42 St

⑬ Take a trip to the **International Center of Photography** and see unique photos from around the world. There are always plenty of good temporary exhibits here.
1114 6th Ave, at 43rd St, www.icp.org, Mon-Fri 9am-7pm, Sat 9am-3pm, Sun 9:30am-1:30pm, $14, B, D, F & M trains to 42 St-Bryant Pk

⑮ The largest branch of the **New York Public Library** opened in 1911 and is located in the Stephen A. Schwarzman Building. In the 1930s, Mayor Fiorello LaGuardia gave the marble lions that sit outside of the building the nicknames

Patience and Fortitude. In doing so he was emphasizing the qualities New Yorkers needed to endure the Depression.

476 5th Ave, at 42nd St, www.nypl.org, Mon, Fri-Sat 10am-6pm, Tue-Wed, Thu 10am-8pm, free, N, Q, R, S, 1, 2 & 3 trains to Times Sq-42 St, B, D, F & M trains to 42 St, 7 train to 5 Av

16 Grand Central Terminal is a Beaux Arts masterpiece embodying the romanticism of train travel. The annual Holiday Laser Light Show, a Christmas-themed light show projected onto the ceiling of the main hall, begins on November 30 and goes on for six weeks. It's very impressive.

89 E 42nd St, between Madison and Lexington avenues, www.grandcentralterminal .com, tel. 212-340-2583, daily 5:30am-2am, S, 4, 5, 6 & 7 trains to Grand Central-42 St

18 The **Chrysler Building** is the crowning achievement of auto industry giant Walter P. Chrysler. Designs of hubcaps and fenders have been incorporated into the building both inside and out. You'll also find waterspouts in the shape of radiator caps. The 1,046-foot-tall (319 meters) building is a unique art deco monument. When it opened in 1930, the Chrysler Building was the tallest building in the world. One year later, it was dethroned by the Empire State Building.

405 Lexington Ave, between 42nd and 43rd streets, not open to the public, S, 4, 5, 6 & 7 trains to Grand Central-42 St

19 The wonderful collection at **The Morgan Library & Museum** comes from wealthy banker and art collector John Pierpont Morgan's own private collection. In 1924, eleven years after his death, it was opened as a public institution. The collection includes manuscripts, drawings, books, and old Middle Eastern tablets, among other things.

225 Madison Ave, at 36th St, www.themorgan.org, tel. 212-685-0008, Tue-Thu 10:30am-5pm, Fri 10:30am-9pm, Sat 10am-6pm, Sun 11am-6pm, $18, 6 train to 33 St, S, 4, 5, 6 & 7 trains to Grand Central

20 The **Empire State Building** is the result of a competition between the chairmen of General Motors and Chrysler to see who could be the first to build the world's tallest building (FYI: General Motors "won"). The pencil-shaped

building opened in 1931 and until 1971 was indeed the tallest building in the world. For those interested in the rankings, the Empire State Building is now the second tallest building in New York and the fourth tallest in the United States. The view from the 86th floor is still as phenomenal as ever.

20 W 34th St, at 5th Ave, www.esbnyc.com, 212-736-3100, daily 8am-2am (last elevators up at 1:15am), $32, 1, 2 & 3 trains to 34 St-Penn Station, B, D, F, N, Q & R trains to 34 St-Herald Sq

㉗ The **Flatiron Building** was designed in 1902 in an attempt to establish a new business district north of Wall Street and sits perfectly on a triangular, iron-shaped plot of land. It's usually windy around the iconic building, so be sure to hold on to your hat.

175 5th Ave, at 23rd St, not open to the public, N & R trains to 23 St

㉘ As a young boy, the 26th president of the United States, Theodore Roosevelt, lived on 20th Street. The **Theodore Roosevelt Birthplace,** a reconstruction of that house, is an interesting place to visit for history buffs and Roosevelt fans alike.

28 E 20th St, between Broadway and Park Ave, www.nps.gov/thrb, tel. 212-260-1616, Tue-Sat 10am-5pm, tours each hour on the hour, free, 6, N & R trains to 23 St

㉛ **Gramercy Park** is the only non-public park in New York. Only residents living in the area have a key. In the 19th century, most apartments were intended for the poor. The apartments at **34 Gramercy Park East** were therefore called "French flats" to distinguish them from those where the working class lived. Go for a drink on the beautiful terrace of the Gramercy Park Hotel.

Between 20th and 21st streets and Park and 3rd avenues, not open to the public, 6 train to 23 St

FOOD & DRINK

❷ Walk into the lobby of Parker New York Hotel and you'll think it's a little bit boring. Then peek behind the red curtain and you'll discover the fabulous retro **Burger Joint.** The concept has something of an underground feel to it. The menu here is simple: hamburger or cheeseburger. Uncomplicated, but oh, so delicious.

119 W 56th St, www.burgerjointny.com/56thstreet, tel. 212-708-7414, Sun-Thu 11am-11:30pm, Fri-Sat 11am-midnight, from $9 (cash only), N, Q & R trains to 57 St-7 Av, F train to 57 St

4 From bustling Lexington Avenue, the smell of fresh coffee will lure you into **Little Collins.** This charming espresso bar is the perfect place to unwind. They make the most delicious espresso in town with milk that's straight from the farm. Hankering for a bite to eat too? Try the "Smash"—tasty avocado and feta on toast.

667 Lexington Ave, www.littlecollinsnyc.com, tel. 212-308-1969, Mon-Fri 7am-5pm, Sat-Sun 8am-4pm, $10, E & M trains to Lexington Av/53 St

7 21 Club stands for all the history and stories that make New York so fantastic. Since 1930 "The 21" has been an institution for "everyone who is anyone," which is made clear by the enormous number of artifacts donated by famous people throughout the years. The jockeys on the façade are proud gifts by Jay van Urk, the Vanderbilts, and many other notables.

21 W 52nd St, www.21club.com, tel. 212-582-7200, Mon-Fri noon-2:30pm & 5:30pm-10pm, Sat 5pm-11pm, $50, E & M trains to 5 Av/53 St

17 Hidden away in Grand Central Terminal you'll find a slice of Scandinavia. With the **Great Northern Food Hall** famous restaurateur Claus Meyer (one of the founders of Noma in Copenhagen) gives New Yorkers what they've been craving: artisanal, barbaric, and organic food. In this food hall you'll find coffee, a bar, a bakery, and hot dogs! Do as the New Yorkers do and go crazy for all these delightful treats.

Grand Central Terminal, Vanderbilt Hall, 89 E 42 St, www.greatnorthernfood.com, tel. 646-568-4020, Mon-Fri 7am-10pm, Sat-Sun 8am-8pm, prices vary by restaurant, 4, 5, 6, 7 & S trains to Grand Central-42 St

21 Hangawi is a Koreatown gem serving traditional vegetarian food, such as rice with avocado and miso sauce in a stone bowl, in a serene space with low,

wooden tables—you must remove your shoes and sit on the floor to eat. It's a wonderful respite from the bustle of the city.

12 E 32nd Street, tel. 212-213-0077, www.hangawirestaurant.com, Mon 5:30pm-10:15pm, Tue & Thu noon-2:30pm & 5:30pm-10:15pm, Fri noon-2:30pm & 5:30pm-10:30pm, Sat 1pm-10:30pm, Sun 5pm-9:30pm, from $20, B, D, F, N, Q & R trains to 34 St-Herald Sq

23 The guys behind Eleven Madison Park opened the fast-casual restaurant **Made Nice.** Here you'll savor the delights and menu items from a three-star restaurant. The chicken with rosemary fries is a definite crowd pleaser.

8 W 28th St, www.madenicenyc.com, tel. 212-887-1677, Mon-Thu 11am-10pm, Fri 11am-9pm, Sat noon-9pm, Sun noon-10pm, $15, R & W trains to 28 St

24 From the roof of **230 Fifth** you can gaze through the palm trees out onto the Empire State Building and lower Manhattan. The atmosphere and view here make having a drink at 230 Fifth a truly unique experience. In the winter, enjoy the same amazing view from inside the bar one floor down.

230 5th Ave, at 27th St, www.230-fifth.com, tel. 212-725-4300, Mon-Fri 2pm-2am, Sat-Sun 10am-2am (21 and up only), $16, cocktails from $14, 6 train to 33 St, B, D, F & M trains to 34 St-Herald Sq

26 On the front of the menu of the classic 1920's diner **Eisenberg's Sandwich Shop** you'll read, "Raising New York's cholesterol since 1929." They serve lime rickeys, egg creams, and of course, pastrami on rye. Little has changed, and that is a good thing.

174 5th Ave, www.eisenbergsnyc.com, tel. 212-675-5096, Mon-Fri 7:30am-6pm, Sat 9am-5pm, Sun 10am-3pm, $10, R & W trains to 23 St

32 Gelato and chocolate at **Venchi** have been known in Italy since 1878 for the quality and delicious flavors. This New York location brings some extras: America's largest chocolate waterfall! This eye-catcher is placed against a wall at the back of the store and attracts at least as much attention as all the goodies at the front.

861 Broadway, https://us.venchi.com, tel. 646-448-8663, Mon-Thur 10am-10:30pm, Fri-Sat 10am-noon, Sun 10am-10pm, N, R, Q, L, 5 & 6 trains to Union Square

SHOPPING

10 Many women in New York City are too busy to scour markets and sift through vintage stores, looking for that one-of-a-kind item they just can't live without. Instead, they head to **Anthropologie** for beautiful, feminine clothing. This concept store also sells a selection of linens and other home goods. Don't forget to check out the store windows—the design team always does an amazing and unique job.

50 Rockefeller Center, www.anthropologie.com, tel. 212-246-0386, Mon-Sat 10am-9pm, Sun 11am-8pm, E & M trains to 5 Av/53 St, B, D, F & M trains to 47-50 Sts-Rockefeller Ctr

22 You'll find the entrance to the **Dover Street Market** down a small street between Park and Lexington avenues. It's easy to shop endlessly in this six-floor store from designer Rei Kawakubo of Comme des Garçons. Items from top fashion labels are beautifully displayed here. Tip: take the elevator all the way to the top, then work your way down floor by floor.

160 Lexington Ave, www.newyork.doverstreetmarket.com, tel. 646-837-7750, Mon-Sat 11am-7pm, Sun noon-6pm, 6 train to 28 St

25 **New York Vintage** is not just any vintage consignment store—it must be the most luxurious one in the world! The first floor is open to the public; the second is almost a private store where you'll find vintage pieces by famous fashion brands that are just for rent. And they let you in only when you're on par with Madonna, Lady Gaga, and Charlize Theron. Luckily the first floor is exciting enough for any vintage shopper.

117 W 25th St, newyorkvintage.com, tel. 212-647-1107, Mon-Sat 11am-7pm, R & W trains to 28 St

29 At first glance **Fishs Eddy** may seem to sell your average dinnerware, but nothing could be further from the truth. Check out the humorous window displays and be sure to control yourself inside—there are some clever designs in this shop. Products include everything from patterned glassware to kitchen towels with iconic NYC buildings on them. This is a great place to pick up nice souvenirs.

889 Broadway, www.fishseddy.com, tel. 212-420-9020, Mon-Sat 10am-9pm, Sun 10am-8pm, N & R trains to 23 St

30 Those with an interest in interior design—or design in general—will not want to miss **ABC Carpet & Home.** The window displays all have unique themes and the style inside is inspiring. The store sells home décor, lifestyle products, jewelry, and of course, furniture. Each floor of the store is styled differently, and always with the latest trends in mind. Downstairs you'll find **ABC Kitchen**—a serene space with amazing food.
888 Broadway, www.abchome.com, tel. 212-473-3000, Mon-Wed & Fri-Sat 10am-7pm, Thu 10am-8pm, Sun 12pm-6pm, N & R trains to 23 St

34 **Beacon's Closet** is a consignment store for hipsters and other bargain hunters who are looking for some serious gems. It's always filled with cool items you won't find anywhere else: from bomber jackets with horse-and-carriage prints and orange camo overalls to haute couture and luxury

brands—all for a steal. Check it out and see if you can find something for either a proper occasion or a fancy-dress party.

10 W 13th St, www.beaconscloset.com, tel. 917-261-4863, daily 11am-8pm, 4, 5, 6, L, N, Q, R & W trains to 14 St-Union Sq

MORE TO EXPLORE

⓫ One of the most popular events at **Radio City Music Hall** is the "Christmas Spectacular" with performances by the Rockettes. Radio City Music Hall is the largest covered theater in the world and is a beautiful example of art deco style.

1260 6th Ave, between 50th and 51st streets, www.radiocity.com, tickets on sale Mon-Sun 11:30am-6pm, see website for programs and prices, B, D, F & M trains to 47-50 Sts-Rockefeller Ctr

⓮ Head to **Bryant Park** for some rest and relaxation. Grab a coffee and a snack at one of the kiosks and then sit back and take in all of the tall buildings around you. At the east edge of the park is one of the city's most popular outdoor bars. In the summer there are open-air movies every Monday night. Until 2010, New York Fashion Week was also held here twice a year, but it has since moved to Lincoln Center.

42nd St and 6th Ave, www.bryantpark.org, daily from 7am, N, Q, R, S, 1, 2 & 3 trains to Times Sq-42 St, B, D, F & M trains to 42 St/7 & 5 Av

㉝ The **Union Square Greenmarket** began in 1976 with a handful of farmers and has since grown into an enormous market where some 140 regional farmers come to sell their products in the peak season. In the winter the market is somewhat smaller. Vendors sell organic fruits and vegetables, bread, cheese, and organic wine. Be sure to also check out the cooking demonstrations from famous local chefs and sample their creations.

E 17th St & Union Square West, www.grownyc.org, Mon, Wed, Fri, Sat 8am-6pm, N, R, Q, L, 5 & 6 trains to Union Square

UPPER EAST SIDE & CENTRAL PARK

ABOUT THE WALK

This is an ideal walk for those with a penchant for art and nature. The route covers what is known as "Museum Mile" and will take you past all of the big museums on the east side of the city, including the Guggenheim and the Met. You'll get to discover amazing art collections and exhibitions. The route will also take you through the beautiful Central Park, where you can escape the hustle and bustle of the city. Head to the park for a nice picnic or bike ride.

THE NEIGHBORHOODS

The stretch of 5th Avenue east of lower **Central Park** is known as Manhattan's "Gold Coast." The area has an incredibly high concentration of private clubs, exclusive schools, and art institutions. No other neighborhood in the country donates as much to national political campaigns as the **Upper East Side.**

The beautiful townhouses that line the avenues and streets near Central Park were once the residences of wealthy businesspeople who made their fortunes in steel, oil, and finance. Today many of these houses are home to cultural institutions, embassies, schools, and museums—although some are still the homes of well-heeled New Yorkers. East of **Park Avenue** the neighborhood is not quite as upscale, more down to earth, and much livelier. On Lexington Avenue you'll find lots of bustling stores and restaurants frequented by young couples and families from the neighborhood.

Those who enjoy museums are in the right place in the Upper East Side. The neighborhood is home to a stretch of 5th Avenue nicknamed "Museum Mile" with such notable museums as the **Metropolitan Museum of Art,** the **Guggenheim,** the **Neue Galerie,** and the **Frick Collection,** which contain some of the most beautiful art collections in the world.

On Madison Avenue you'll find countless galleries, jewelers, and exclusive stores and boutiques from top designers. The department stores **Barneys** and **Bloomingdale's** are also located here, and avid shoppers can regularly be spotted walking down the street with their little and big brown bags.

SHORT ON TIME? HERE ARE THE HIGHLIGHTS:
13 HECKSCHER BALLFIELDS + 26 GUGGENHEIM MUSEUM + 27 NEUE GALERIE + 29 METROPOLITAN MUSEUM OF ART + 31 THE LOEB BOATHOUSE

TIPS
// This walk offers a good mix of art and nature
// The perfect activity for a Sunday
// The walk can be broken into parts

UPPER EAST SIDE & CENTRAL PARK

1. Bloomingdale's
2. Sprinkles Cupcake ATM
3. The Bar Room
4. Barneys
5. Metropolitan Club
6. The Pierre
7. Knickerbocker Club
8. Edith and Ernesto Fabbri House
9. 726 Madison Avenue
10. Match 65 Brasserie
11. Central Park Zoo
12. Wollman Rink
13. **Heckscher Ballfields**
14. Roosevelt House
15. East Pole Restaurant
16. 7th Regiment Armory
17. West side of Park Avenue, from 68th to 69th streets
18. Creel and Gow
19. Frick Collection
20. Christian Louboutin
21. Café Carlyle
22. Butterfield Market
23. La Maison du Chocolat
24. The Jewish Museum
25. Cooper Hewitt Smithsonian Design Museum
26. **Guggenheim Museum**
27. **Neue Galerie**
28. 1040 5th Avenue
29. **Metropolitan Museum of Art**
30. E.A.T.
31. **The Loeb Boathouse**
32. Bethesda Fountain/Bethesda Terrace
33. Naumburg Bandshell/ The Mall

LEGEND

- >> SIGHTS & ATTRACTIONS
- >> FOOD & DRINK
- >> SHOPPING
- >> MORE TO EXPLORE
- >> WALK HIGHLIGHT

Subway Line — Times Square — Station Name

WALK 4 DESCRIPTION (approx. 6.3 mi/10 km)

Start on Lexington Avenue with some shopping at Bloomingdale's ❶, then get a cupcake out of the cupcake ATM ❷. Walk back and turn right on 60th Street, past a bar and restaurant that would be a good place to remember for the evening ❸. Continue walking and turn right on Madison Avenue for some shopping ❹. Then continue on to 60th Street ❺ and turn right at Central Park for afternoon tea and a private club ❻ ❼. Turn right on 62nd Street to number 11 ❽. Then go left on Madison Avenue and check out number 726 ❾. Continue on to 65th Street for a nice lunch ❿. Or turn left on 64th Street and walk into Central Park, the backyard for every New Yorker ⓫ ⓬ ⓭. Leave the park at 65th Street ⓮ and continue on for another great lunch spot ⓯. Turn left on Lexington Avenue, left again, and then right for some alternative art ⓰ and the west side of Park Avenue ⓱. Turn right on 70th Street for bric-a-brac ⓲ and back toward the park for the Frick Collection ⓳. Go right on 5th Avenue along Central Park, then right on 73rd Street, and left on Madison Avenue for shoe (and window) shopping ⓴. Turn right on 76th Street for a nice meal—Upper East side style ㉑. Head left on Lexington Avenue and pick up some delicious food for a picnic ㉒. Then turn left on 78th Street and right on Madison Avenue for some heavenly chocolate ㉓. Take a right on 79th and then a left and stroll along Park Avenue. At 84th Street turn left back to Madison Avenue for some more shopping. Continue to 93rd Street and turn left. At 5th Avenue turn left past several of the city's most famous museums ㉔ ㉕ ㉖ ㉗ and be sure to also keep an eye out for number 1040 5th Avenue ㉘. The last museum you'll pass is the Metropolitan Museum of Art ㉙. Then take a detour to Madison Avenue, between 81st and 80th streets for a little break and something good to eat ㉚. Head back to 5th Avenue and turn right on 79th Street into Central Park again for a drink and something to eat ㉛ along the water. End the day by checking out the Bethesda Fountain and Terrace ㉜ and then walk over to the Naumburg Bandshell ㉝.

SIGHTS & ATTRACTIONS

⑤ In 1891 the **Metropolitan Club** was established under the chairmanship of banker J. P. Morgan. It is a private club, and the building was inspired by the architecture of Italian palazzos. The inside, which is unfortunately accessible only to members, is extravagantly decorated with Corinthian columns, rich red carpets, marble, and velvet.

1 E 60th St, at 5th Ave, not open to the public, N, Q & R trains to 5 Av/59 St

⑦ The **Knickerbocker Club** is another of the many private clubs on 5th Avenue. The building dates from 1913 and was designed by the American architects Delano & Aldrich. Stylistically the building's architecture includes a mixture of Georgian and Federal elements.

805 5th Ave, not open to the public, N, Q & R trains to 5 Av/59 St

⑧ At 11 East 62nd Street, you'll find the **Edith and Ernesto Fabbri House.** Edith Shepard Fabbri received this amazing house as a gift from her parents when she married banker Ernesto Fabbri. Edith's mother was a member of the wealthy Vanderbilt family.

11 E 62nd St, between 5th and Madison avenues, not open to the public, N, Q & R trains to 5 Av/59 St

⑨ **726 Madison Avenue** was built in 1932 for the Bank of Manhattan Company. The building's Georgian-style architecture had not been in fashion for nearly a century, and as a result, it seems completely out of place on this posh street.

726 Madison Ave, at 64th St, not open to the public, 6 train to 68th Street/Hunter College, F train to Lexington Av/63 St

⑭ The **Roosevelt House** is actually two houses with one shared entrance. Sarah Delano Roosevelt gave the house to her son Franklin and his new bride, Eleanor, and the dominating mother lived at number 47. In 1921 and 1922, FDR and his wife lived at number 49 while he was recovering from polio. The house always remained their home base whenever they were in New York. Following Sarah's death in 1941, the house was sold.

47-49 E 65th St, between Madison and Park avenues, www.roosevelthouse.hunter
.cuny.edu, tel. 212-650-3174, not open to the public, tours by request, Sat set tours at
10am, noon & 2pm, 6 train to 68 St-Hunter College

⑯ The **7th Regiment Armory,** also known as Park Avenue Armory, seems a bit
like a fort. The large brick building was once the headquarters of the seventh
regiment of the New York National Guard. The interior is beautifully decorated,
but after 120 years, the building, which dates back to 1880, had grown
dilapidated. In 2006 the Park Armory Conservancy began significant renovations
to transform the building into a unique place for unconventional art.
643 Park Ave, between 66th and 67th streets, www.armoryonpark.org, open during
exhibitions, see website for exhibition times and prices, tours on request, 6 train to
68 St-Hunter College

⑰ The houses on the **west side of Park Avenue, from 68th to 69th streets,**
were saved from demolition in 1965 by Marquesa de Cuevas, a member of the
wealthy Rockefeller family. She donated the buildings to her favorite charities,
including the Americas Society, the Spanish Institute, and the Istituto Italiano di
Cultura. Today you can come here for exhibits, readings, and classes.
Park Ave, between 68th and 69th streets, 6 train to 68 St-Hunter College

⑲ The **Frick Collection** is located in the former home of the Pittsburgh steel
magnate Henry Clay Frick. The collection includes masterpieces from many
famous European artists, such as Van Eyck, Bellini, Titian, and Goya. Today the
museum maintains the same homey feel as when Frick himself lived here.
1 E 70th St, at 5th Ave, www.frick.org, tel. 212-288-0700, Tue-Sat 10am-6pm, Sun
11am-5pm, $20, 6 train to 68 St-Hunter College

㉔ **The Jewish Museum** began in 1904 with 26 objects on display for visitors to
view. Today the collection has grown to include 26,000 objects that reflect
4,000 years of Jewish art and culture. You'll find everything from archeological
artifacts and paintings to videos and interactive websites.
1109 5th Ave, at 92nd St, www.thejewishmuseum.org, tel. 212-475-4880, Mon-Tue &
Fri-Sun 11am-5:45pm, Thu 11am-8pm, $15, free on Saturdays, 6 train to 96 St

25 The former home of the famous philanthropist and steel magnate Andrew Carnegie was transformed into the **Cooper Hewitt Smithsonian Design Museum** in 1977. Visit the museum to see everything from historic to contemporary design, and from one-of-a-kind to mass-produced design objects.
2 E 91st St, at 5th Ave, www.cooperhewitt.org, tel. 212-849-2950, Sun-Fri 10am-6pm, Sat 10am-9pm, $16, Sat from 6pm voluntary donation, 6 train to 96 St

26 The **Guggenheim Museum** is one of the most famous buildings by architect Frank Lloyd Wright, and the building's unique architecture is certainly at least as important at the Picassos and Kandinskys hanging inside. For the ultimate experience, take the elevator to the top and then work your way downward. Plan to spend at least half a day in the museum. Tip: on Saturdays from 5:45pm to 7:45pm, you pay what you want to enter.
1071 5th Ave, at 89th St, www.guggenheim.org, tel. 212-423-3500, Sun-Mon & Wed-Fri 10am-5:45pm, Tue & Sat 10am-8pm, $25, 4, 5 & 6 trains to 86 St

27 The **Neue Galerie** is devoted to German and Austrian art. This building in which the museum is housed was previously the home of Mrs. Cornelius Vanderbilt, a society doyenne and the widow of one of the richest men in New York. Today, in addition to the museum, the building also houses two excellent cafés.
1048 5th Ave, at 86th St, www.neuegalerie.org, Thu-Mon 11am-6pm, $20, 4, 5 & 6 trains to 86 St/Lexington Av, B & C trains to 86 St/Central Park West

28 A year after her husband was assassinated in Dallas, former First Lady Jacqueline Kennedy Onassis moved to the 15th floor at **1040 5th Avenue.** She thoroughly valued and appreciated the anonymity afforded her by the people of NYC and often went for walks in Central Park. Jackie lived here until her death in 1994.
1040 5th Ave, not open to the public, 4, 5 & 6 trains to 86 St

29 The grand building that houses the **Metropolitan Museum of Art** (the Met) bears a strong resemblance to the Palace of Versailles. In this museum you'll find artwork from ancient times as well as modern art. Various additions have

been made to the building over the years, but the 5th Avenue side dates back to 1895-1902. For a nice view, head up to the rooftop garden.

1000 5th Ave, at 82nd St, www.metmuseum.org, tel. 212-535-7710, Sat-Thu 10am-5:30pm, Fri-Sat 10am-9pm, $25 (suggested), 6 train to 77 St, 4, 5 & 6 trains to 86 St

32 The **Bethesda Fountain** is the backdrop of many wedding photos. Brides and grooms come here nearly every day to pose for pictures. Rightly so—this is an especially beautiful spot with the lake, rowboats, and grand buildings of western Manhattan in the background. **Bethesda Terrace** was one of the first structures in Central Park. The terrace has two levels, which are connected by stately steps. Be sure to walk underneath and admire the gorgeous tiled ceiling.

Terrace Dr, in Central Park, www.centralpark.com, daily 7am-1am, B & C trains to 72 St, 6 train to 77 St

33 The neoclassical **Naumburg Bandshell** was built in Central Park in 1923. Since then, artists of all ilk have performed here. Famous people such as Martin Luther King Jr. and John Lennon have also stood on this stage. Find out about performances here on the Central Park website. **The Mall** runs through the middle of the park, from the Bethesda Terrace down to 66th Street. There are plenty of benches along the Mall, but you may have to compete with the street artists, roller skaters, and skateboarders to get one.

Central Park, between E 70th and E 71st streets, www.centralpark.com, 6 train to 68 St-Hunter College

FOOD & DRINK

3 Behind the brown doors at the **Bar Room** hide an old-style bar and restaurant. A beautiful mural decorates the back room, while a long bar in the front room invites guest to sit and enjoy a cocktail with friends. Or colleagues, for that matter, since this is a popular spot to stop for drinks on the way home from work. The food here is simple but good, and the Bar Room Burger is a favorite.

117 E 60th St, www.thebarroomnyc.com, tel. 212-561-5523, Mon & Sun 11am-1am, Tue-Sat 11am-2am, $24, N, Q & R trains to Lexington Av

6 Since 1930, **The Pierre** has been one of the most elegant hotels in New York City. Treat yourself to afternoon tea at the Two E Bar/Lounge here.
2 E 61st St, www.thepierreny.com, tel. 212-838-8000, daily for afternoon tea 3pm-6pm, $55, N & R trains to 5 Av/59 St

10 **Match 65 Brasserie** is classical Paris in the heart of the Upper East Side. Thanks to their great ambience and fantastic food, the walls are lined with awards, among which there is one for the best tuna tartare in New York.
29 E 65th St, www.match65.com, tel. 212-737-4400, Mon-Fri 11:30am-11pm, Sat 11am-11pm, Sun 11am-10pm, $22, 6 train to 68 St

15 Located in the middle of the Upper East Side, **East Pole Restaurant** is a popular spot among hip locals. It is the sister restaurant of The Fat Radish on the Lower East Side, so you can expect the same levels of quality and service and the same prices at both locations. Vegetable dishes such as the roasted parsnips and the walnut and beet hummus are great appetizers. This restaurant is an excellent spot for lunch.
133 E 65th St, www.theeastpolenyc.com, tel. 212-249-2222, Mon-Fri 11:30am-3pm & 5:30pm-midnight, Sat 10:30am-midnight, Sun 10:30am-11pm, $28, F train to Lexington Av/63 St

22 The **Butterfield Market** has been a neighborhood fixture for more than a century. Everything at this local market is made fresh, and they have delicious coffee, sandwiches, fruit, and cakes. Tip: buy lunch here, then walk over to Central Park for a nice picnic like the locals do. Don't forget to pick up some homemade frozen yogurt for along the way.
1114 Lexington Ave, www.butterfieldnyc.com, Mon-Fri 7am-8pm, Sat-Sun 8am-5pm, 4, 5 & 6 trains to 86 St

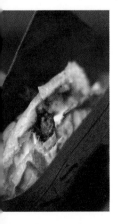

30 E.A.T. is the ideal place to come for a delicious salad or sandwich to refuel after walking through the streets, shops, and museums along this route.

1064 Madison Ave, between 80th and 81st streets, www.elizabar.com, tel. 212-772-0022, daily 7am-9pm, $16, 6 train to 77th Street, 4, 5 & 6 trains to 86 St

31 The Loeb Boathouse is a great colonial-style restaurant on the water in Central Park. Next to the restaurant, you can enjoy a drink at the Boat Bar and watch as people row past. This is a nice place to end the day.

E 72nd St, Park Dr N, www.thecentralparkboathouse.com, tel. 212-517-2233, Mon-Fri noon-4pm, Sat-Sun 9:30am-4pm (times change during the high and low seasons), $25, 6 train to 68 St-Hunter College

SHOPPING

1 Shopping, shopping, shopping is what **Bloomingdale's** is all about. For decades New Yorkers have been coming to this department store to take advantage of all that the worlds of beauty and fashion have to offer. Curious about what's in all of those little and big brown bags you see on the street? Then stop inside. Don't expect to be able to see everything in the store though—it's big. Take a good look at the map, too, because it's easy to get lost in here.

1000 3rd Ave, between 59th St and Lexington Ave, www.bloomingdales.com, tel. 212-705-2000, Mon-Wed 11am-8:30pm, Thu-Sat 10am-10pm, Sun 10am-9pm, 4, 5, 6, N, Q & R trains to 59 St

2 Sprinkles Cupcake ATM is something you won't want to miss. Delicious cupcakes are available 24 hours a day from this cheerfully colored machine. It's a pleasant twist on your average vending machine. All cupcakes are handmade in the shop next door.

780 Lexington Ave, between 60th and 61st streets, www.sprinkles.com, tel. 212-207-8375, Mon-Sat 9am-9pm, Sun 10am-8pm, from $4.25, 4, 5, 6, N, Q & R trains to 59 St

❹ **Barneys** started out selling men's suits and has expanded to one of the most distinguished stores in all of NYC. Here you'll find designers and brands that you won't find in any other department store. Upper East Side moms—or their personal shoppers—come here to get fancy dresses for their little ones. If you're feeling inspired by the sophisticated style of the locals in this neighborhood, then stop by for some additions to your wardrobe—just be sure your credit card limit is high enough.

660 Madison Ave, at 60th St, www.barneys.com, tel. 212-826-8900, Mon-Fri 10am-9pm, Sat 10am-7pm, Sun 11am-7pm, N, Q & R trains to 5 Av/59 St

❽ **Creel and Gow** offers an impressive selection of bric-a-brac and feels more like a museum than a shop. You can spend hours wandering around and talking to the friendly owner.

131 E 70th St, www.creelandgow.com, tel. 212-327-4281, Mon-Sat 10am-6pm, 6 train to 68 St

❷⓿ **Christian Louboutin** designs striking shoes and handbags recognizable by their characteristic red soles. In this store you'll find all of his designs in one place. Beware, the shoes also come with a hefty price tag.

965 Madison Ave, at 74th St, www.christianlouboutin.com, open Mon-Sat 10am-6pm, 6 train to 77 St

❷❸ **La Maison du Chocolat** takes chocolate very seriously. Everything you buy here has been imported from Paris. Fortunately, it is also possible to order this chocolate online, because once you've tasted it, you'll never want anything else.

1018 Madison Ave, between 78th and 79th streets, www.lamaisonduchocolat.us, tel. 212-744-7117, Mon-Sat 10am-7pm, Sun 11am-6pm, 6 train to 77 St

MORE TO EXPLORE

11 The **Central Park Zoo** is home to a number of NYC's most beloved inhabitants. The polar bears and sea lions are among the most popular here. Come see if any of the main characters from DreamWorks's *Madagascar* have máde it back home yet.

Central Park, near 64th St at 5th Ave, www.centralparkzoo.com, April-Nov Mon-Fri 10am-5pm, Sat-Sun 10am-5:30pm, Nov-April daily 10am-4:30pm, $18, N, Q & R trains to 5 Av/59 St

12 Ice skating at **Wollman Rink** has long been a favorite pastime for many New York City residents. Glide across the ice here from fall until spring. Then from July until September the Victoria Gardens amusement park moves in.

Central Park, near 59th St and 6th Ave, www.wollmanskatingrink.com, tel. 212-439-6900, daily from 10am, Mon-Thu $11.25, Fri-Sun $18, skate rental $8, N, Q & R trains to 5 Av, A, B, C, D & 1 trains to 59 St/Columbus Circle

13 **Heckscher Ballfields** has six softball and baseball diamonds, and there's nearly always a team out there practicing or a game going on. Take a seat and watch but be sure to look up from time to time to appreciate the contrast between Central Park and the rest of Manhattan that surrounds it.

Near 63rd St Central, www.centralpark.com, daily 6am-1am, F train to Lexington Av/63 St

21 Anyone who thinks cabaret is a thing of the past definitely ought to come to **Café Carlyle** for a dinner show. Café Carlyle is located in the Carlyle Hotel.

Carlyle Hotel, 35 E 76th St, at Madison Ave, www.cafecarlylenewyork.com, tel. 212-744-1600, Sept-June Mon-Sat 6pm-1am, $165 for a seat, $120 at the bar, 6 train to 77 St

WALK **5**

UPPER WEST SIDE & HARLEM

ABOUT THE WALK

This long walk focuses on African American culture and historical architecture. The route travels along the Hudson River through the picturesque Riverside Park. It is very calm in and around the park, and you'll get to see a very different side of New York City. The last part of the walk will take you through Harlem, which is best to visit on a weekday because it can be really busy here on the weekend.

THE NEIGHBORHOODS

Between Central Park and the Hudson River lies the **Upper West Side,** a neighborhood known for its rich intellectual and cultural history. Today it is hard to imagine that, up until the 19th century, this part of New York City was considered the wilderness. The area wasn't built up until after 1880, when construction began on the first apartment complex—the **Dakota.** As more train lines were laid, it became easier for New Yorkers to live farther away from their work downtown. Thus, the Upper West Side was born.

With the brownstones and townhouses, many streets in the neighborhood are historical sites. The southern part of the Upper West Side is a cultural hub, and in the north, the skyline is dominated by **Riverside Church** and **Columbia University.** In between you'll find a mix of small museums, neighborhood shops, nice boutiques, and good restaurants.

Along the banks of the Hudson River stretches **Riverside Park.** According to local residents, this is Manhattan's most beautiful park, and locals come here for sports and leisure, and for the cool breeze off the Hudson during the hot city summers.

North of the Upper West Side lies an important center of African American culture: **Harlem.** Here you'll find art galleries, churches (often named after notable African American figures), the legendary **Apollo Theater,** and much more. In recent years

Harlem has experienced a wave of gentrification, and the neighborhood's historical brownstones and wide streets have been attracting people from around the city.

Upper North Harlem is a bit grittier, so keep that in mind. The neighborhood is never quiet—there is music all around, and people regularly sit out on the steps in front of their homes and converse loudly. Here you can experience the true spirit of Harlem.

SHORT ON TIME? HERE ARE THE HIGHLIGHTS:
4 THE DAKOTA + 13 RIVERSIDE PARK + 18 COLUMBIA UNIVERSITY + 24 APOLLO THEATER + 28 RED ROOSTER HARLEM

TIPS
// Think this walk is a little long? You can easily split it in two
// The stretch along the Hudson is great for biking
// This route can also be done in reverse

UPPER WEST SIDE & HARLEM

1. ABC television studios
2. Columbus Avenue between W 68th & W 72nd streets
3. Dark Bullet
4. **The Dakota**
5. Strawberry Fields
6. Levain Bakery
7. Piccolo Café
8. Aylsmere apartments
9. West 76th Street
10. American Museum of Natural History
11. Amorino
12. Boat Basin Café
13. **Riverside Park**
14. Nicolas Roerich Museum
15. Tom's Restaurant
16. General Grant National Memorial
17. Riverside Church
18. **Columbia University**
19. Alma Mater
20. Low Memorial Library
21. Cathedral Church of Saint John the Divine
22. Hungarian Pastry Shop
23. Morningside Park
24. **Apollo Theater**
25. Studio Museum
26. National Jazz Museum in Harlem
27. Astor Row
28. **Red Rooster Harlem**
29. Vinatería
30. Double Dutch Espresso
31. Lido
32. Harlem Tavern
33. Silvana
34. The Ravine/The Loch

WALK 5 DESCRIPTION (approx. 10 mi/16 km)

Begin at ABC television studios ❶. Head north on Columbus Avenue and shop in some nice boutiques ❷. Then turn left on 72nd Street for sake ❸ or turn right and walk past the building where John Lennon once lived ❹. Cross the street and go into Central Park. Immediately after you enter, there is a path that leads to Strawberry Fields ❺. Walk back and turn right on Central Park West. Take a left on 74th Street for cookies ❻, then a right and a right again for a bite to eat in 75th Street ❼. Turn left on Columbus Avenue and then right on 76th Street to see some unique buildings ❽ ❾. Continue straight to Central Park West and then turn left to visit a museum ❿. Head left down 81st Street and left on Amsterdam Ave for ice cream and coffee ⓫. Take a right on 80th Street to Riverside Drive and make a left, then at 79th Street make a right into the park. Walk straight to the Boat Basin Café ⓬ then under the roundabout. Enjoy a drink by the water, then walk through Riverside Park, keeping the Hudson River on your left ⓭. Take the tunnel under the road at 83rd Street and continue through the park. Cross 95th Street and continue on the path down to the left and then to the right back into the park. This long walk will take you up along some sports fields. At the last field, walk up and out of the park. Walk back in the direction you came from, then turn left on 107th Street for Russian art ⓮. Take a left on Broadway to see a famous New York City diner ⓯. Go left on 113th Street and, at the end, make a right on Riverside Drive to visit a tomb and a church ⓰ ⓱. Take a right on Claremont Avenue, then left on 120th Street, and then right on Broadway toward the entrance to Columbia University ⓲ ⓳ ⓴. Walk across the campus to Amsterdam Avenue, take a right, and continue straight to see a church and have a drink ㉑ ㉒. Walk back up Amsterdam Avenue and turn right on 113th Street toward Morningside Park ㉓. Walk through the park and then go left on Manhattan Avenue. Turn right on 125th Street to the musical heart of Harlem and take in some culture and art ㉔ ㉕. Walk back a bit and take a right on Adam Clayton Powell Jr. Blvd and right again onto 129th Street for jazz history ㉖. Take a left on 5th Avenue and right to Astor Row ㉗. Turn left again on Malcolm X Boulevard for soul food ㉘. Take a right on 120th Street and then left on Frederick Douglass Boulevard ㉙ ㉚ ㉛ ㉜ ㉝. If you're still up for seeing some nature at this point, continue on to The Loch ㉞.

SIGHTS & ATTRACTIONS

1 The ABC television network is responsible for programs such as *Modern Family*, *General Hospital*, and *Desperate Housewives*. At **ABC television studios** on the Upper West Side you can look into the studio from the street during news programs. Maybe you'd like to be part of the studio audience during a *Live with Kelly and Ryan* morning show? Then get your tickets in advance online or try your luck in the standby line starting at 7am.

77 W 66th St, https://abc.go.com and www.kellyandryan.com, free, 1 train to 66 St

4 **The Dakota** dates back to 1884 and is actually nothing more than an upscale apartment building. However, since December 8, 1980, when John Lennon was shot dead in the street on the way back to his home here, people flock to this building. To this day, Lennon's wife, Yoko Ono, still lives in the Dakota. With its turrets and spires, the building resembles something of a castle. This was done intentionally to convince wealthy New Yorkers that living in an apartment could be just as luxurious as an entire house.

1 W 72nd St, not open to the public, B, C, 1, 2 & 3 trains to 72 St

5 Following John Lennon's death, **Strawberry Fields,** a small spot in Central Park across from the Dakota, has become a place to pay respects to the musician. Fans come to here to place flowers on a memorial mosaic bearing the single word "imagine." This peaceful spot in the park is a nice place to sit and listen as fans sing and play the guitar in tribute to Lennon.

Entrance to Central Park West on W 72nd St, www.centralparknyc.org, tel. 212-310-6600, daily 6am-1am, B, C, 1, 2 & 3 trains to 72 St

6 The **Aylsmere apartments** are located in a beautiful Renaissance building decorated with brick ornaments. The building dates back to 1894 and was built as apartments for the wealthy. Initially there were just two apartments per floor, complete with dining rooms, sitting rooms, bedrooms, bathrooms, and—of course—a room for the help. Following the Great Depression, however, the apartments were split up.

60 W 76th St, not open to the public, 1, 2, 3, B & C trains to 72 St

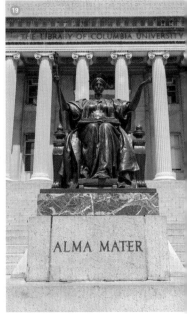

9 This part of **West 76th Street** gives a good picture of the beautiful townhouses and rowhouses that are so typical of the Upper West Side. This style house commonly appears in the movies and on TV. Most homes on this street were built between 1887 and 1898.

W 76th St between Columbus Ave and Central Park West, B & C trains to 81 St-Museum of Natural History

10 The **American Museum of Natural History** is one of the biggest museums in the United States and is primarily known for its large collection of dinosaur fossils. The stately museum, which is located across from Central Park, has impressive collections on Native Americans, human biology and evolution, meteorites, minerals, mammals, and much, much more.

Central Park West, at W 79th St, www.amnh.org, tel. 212-769-5100, daily 10am-5:45pm, $22 (or voluntary donation), B & C trains to 81 St, 1 train to 79 St

14 The **Nicolas Roerich Museum** is a small, eccentric museum in a typical Upper West Side townhouse. The Russian artist came to New York City in the 1920s, and this museum displays some 200 pieces of his work. Cards and reproductions of his artwork are also available for purchase here.

319 W 107th St, www.roerich.org, tel. 212-864-7752, Tue-Fri noon-5pm, Sat-Sun 2pm-5pm, voluntary donation, 1 train to Cathedral Parkway, B & C trains to Cathedral Pkwy (110 St)

15 Characters in the popular comedy *Seinfeld* regularly ate at the fictional Monk's Café. The inside of the café was a studio, but images of the exterior were of **Tom's Restaurant.** The neon sign above this restaurant is now one of the most recognized in the city. Suzanne Vega's hit song "Tom's Diner" is also based on this restaurant.

2880 Broadway, www.tomsrestaurant.net, tel. 212-864-6137, Sun-Wed 6am-1:30am, Thu-Sat 24 hours, $10, 1 train to 110 St

16 The 18th president, General Ulysses S. Grant, and his wife, Julia, were laid to rest at the **General Grant National Memorial** but not technically buried in the tomb. Thus, an old student's riddle asks, "Who is buried in Grant's Tomb?" The

answer, of course, is nobody. A Civil War hero, Grant was very popular in his time, which explains why his is the largest mausoleum in North America.
122nd St and Riverside Dr, www.grantstomb.org, tel. 646-670-7251, Thu-Sun 10am-11am, noon-1pm, 2pm-3pm & 4pm-5pm, free, 1 & 9 trains to 116 St

🅐 Standing 392 feet tall (120 meters), **Riverside Church,** which was completed in 1930, is the tallest church in the United States. The building was modeled on the Gothic cathedral of Chartres in France. Inside the church hangs a carillon with 74 bells—the heaviest in the world. The largest bell weighs 18 tons, and the smallest just 11 pounds.
490 Riverside Dr, www.theriversidechurchny.org, tel. 212-870-6700, daily 7am-10pm, free, 1 train to 116 St

🅐 **Columbia University** is one of the oldest, wealthiest, and largest universities in the country, not to mention it's a prestigious Ivy League school. In 1897, the university moved to its current location in Morningside Heights. The hustle and bustle here, combined with a mix of classic and modern architecture and an abundance of green space make this a truly urban campus. Among the impressive list of famous Columbia alumni, you'll find Theodore Roosevelt, John Jay, and Barack Obama.
W 114th to 120th streets, from Broadway to Amsterdam Ave, www.columbia.edu, tel. 212-854-1754, free, 1 train to 116 St

🅐 The most photographed item on the Columbia University campus is probably the bronze **Alma Mater** statue. With her outstretched arms and an open book on her lap, she appears to be welcoming students and visitors. Hidden among the folds of her robe is an owl, the symbol of wisdom. Legend has it that the first student of each incoming class to find the owl will graduate at the top of the class.
W 116th St, between Broadway and Amsterdam Ave, 1 train to 116 St

🅐 **Low Memorial Library** is a classical building dating back to 1895. The building, with its dome-shaped roof and row of columns in front, is located in the middle of the Columbia University campus. Despite the name, the building has not housed a library since 1934. Instead, it is home to a number of school

offices as well as the Visitors Center (office 213), where you can pick up a map of campus. For those interested in the university's rich history, there is a collection of artifacts on display in the building's lobby.

535 W 116th St, between Broadway and Amsterdam Ave, Mon-Fri 9am-5pm, free, 1 train to 116 St

㉑ If bigger is indeed better, then you may never find a better cathedral than the **Cathedral Church of Saint John the Divine.** Construction of this colossus, which began in 1891 and is still not complete, has been a truly time-consuming affair. Every April dozens of cyclists come to the church for the traditional blessing of the bikes. Tours of the cathedral are offered daily.

1047 Amsterdam Ave, www.stjohndivine.org, daily 7:30am-6pm, check website for tour times and prices, free, 1 train to 110 St

㉕ When **Studio Museum** opened in 1968, it was the first museum in the country dedicated to promoting the work of African American artists. In this museum, which actually feels more like a gallery or studio, you can check out artwork from the 19th and 20th centuries by African American artists or artists influenced by black culture. In addition to the permanent collection, the museum also has temporary exhibits, such as—for example—historical photos of the Harlem Renaissance in the 1920s.

429 W 127th St, www.studiomuseum.org, Thu-Fri noon-9pm, Sat 10am-6pm, Sun noon-6pm, voluntary donation, free on Sundays, 2 & 3 trains to 125 St

㉗ **Astor Row** refers to the 28 townhouses on the south side of West 130th Street in Harlem. Designed by Charles Buek and built between 1880 and 1883, the houses were very progressive for their time. Each one is three stories, set back about 20 feet (6 meters) from the road and has a beautiful wooden porch. However, many of the porches are no longer originals due to necessary renovations.

W 130th St, between 5th Ave and Lenox Ave, 2 & 3 trains to 125 St

FOOD & DRINK

❸ Real sake connoisseurs will love to visit New York—especially **Dark Bullet:** the New York sake and oyster bar in the Upper West Side. They have an unfathomable amount of sakes, *shōchūs*, and Japanese whiskeys on the menu. A fantastic night out is guaranteed.
154 W 72nd St, www.darkbullet.com, tel. 212-235-6788, daily 12:30pm-1am, sake from $15, 1,2,3 trains to 72 St

❻ Early in the morning you can already smell the scent of freshly baked cookies throughout the street. **Levain Bakery** is especially known for its chocolate chip walnut cookies. The line is often all the way out the door, but the cookies are well worth the wait.
167 W 74th St, www.levainbakery.com, tel. 917-464-3769, Mon-Sat 8am-7pm, Sun 9am-7pm, cookies from $5, 1, 2 & 3 trains to 72 St

❼ This restaurant is tiny but cozy. All day long **Piccolo Café** serves—among other things—breakfast sandwiches with complimentary coffee. This is a good place to come for a quick bite during lunch or at night for dinner. At the window outside you can also get coffee to go.
313 Amsterdam Ave, www.piccolocafe.us, tel. 212-873-0962, Mon-Fri 5pm-11pm, Sat-Sun 11am-5pm, $10, 1, 2 & 3 trains to 72 St

⓫ Who said ice cream is just for kids? **Amorino** is the best ice cream shop in the Upper West Side where you can choose your own combination or pick a flavor combination paired by the owners. They serve beautiful rose-shaped scoops, so—if only for a short while—you do feel like a child again.
414 Amsterdam Ave, www.amorino.com, tel. 212-887-5700, Mon-Thu noon-10pm, Fri noon-11pm, Sat-Sun 10am-11pm, from $5, 1 train to 79 St

⓬ After walking through Riverside Park, find a table at the **Boat Basin Café** and relax a bit. Drink in hand, you can look out over the marina, the Hudson, and New Jersey as you watch the sun set. This casual outdoor restaurant is

open when the weather is nice. The locals especially like to come here in the summer when a cool breeze blows in off the water.

W 79th St near the Hudson River, www.boatbasincafe.com, tel. 212-496-5542, late March-late Oct Mon-Wed noon-11pm, Thu-Sat noon-11:30pm, Sun noon-10pm, $11, 1 train to 79 St

㉒ In the shadow of the Cathedral of Saint John the Divine stands the **Hungarian Pastry Shop.** This spot is such a favorite among Columbia University students that you'd almost say it was part of the school's campus. However, other neighborhood residents also like to come here for the good selection of pastries and a cup of coffee.

1030 Amsterdam Ave, at 111th St, tel. 212-866-4230, Mon-Fri 7:30am-11:30pm, Sat 8:30am-11:30pm, Sun 8:30am-10:30pm, coffee from $3 (cash only), 1 train to Cathedral Pkwy (110th St)

㉘ Red Rooster Harlem serves up classic soul food: simple but delicious Southern fare. The fried yardbird, in particular, is highly recommended. The restaurant is always busy, and there's often live music at the bar. Downstairs,

Ginny's Supper Club is tucked away. If you can't get a table at Red Rooster, you may be able to find a spot at Ginny's.

310 Malcolm X Blvd, www.redroosterharlem.com, tel. 212-792-9001, Mon-Thu 11:30am-10:30pm, Fri 7pm-11:30pm, Sat 10am-11:30pm, Sun 10am-10pm, $27, 2 & 3 trains to 125 St/Lenox Av, A, B, C & D trains to 125 St/St Nicholas Av

29 Everything you see in the trendy restaurant **Vinatería** is secondhand and has been repurposed to give it a new life. At the big bar they serve delicious cocktails, and the food in the restaurant is traditional Spanish-Italian fare made primarily with local, seasonal products.

2211 Frederick Douglass Blvd, www.vinaterianyc.com, tel. 212-662-8462, Mon 5pm-10pm, Tue-Thu 5pm-11pm, Fri 11am-midnight, Sat-Sun 11am-10pm, $22, B, C, 2 & 3 trains to 116 St

30 A local coffeehouse in Harlem is something of a rare gem. At **Double Dutch Espresso** you can get a shot of coffee, along with something yummy to eat, of course. In the summer, sit on the nice terrace out back.

2194 Frederick Douglass Blvd, www.doubledutchespresso.com, tel. 646-429-8834, Mon-Fri 7am-8pm, Sat-Sun 8am-8pm, $3, B, C, 2 & 3 trains to 116 St

31 **Lido** is a favorite Italian restaurant for many downtown New Yorkers. This is mostly thanks to the pure food made with organic, seasonal products. The restaurant is set up old-school Italian style and has a nice terrace outside. Renowned chef Serena Bass and owner Susannah welcome you with open arms here.

2168 Frederick Douglass Blvd, www.lidoharlem.com, tel. 646-490-8575, Mon-Thu 11:30am-4pm & 5pm-10pm, Fri 11:30am-4pm & 5pm-11pm, Sat 10:30am-4pm & 5pm-11pm, Sun 10:30am-4pm & 5pm-10pm, $21, B, C, 2 & 3 trains to 116 St

32 The **Harlem Tavern** restaurant and beer garden is known locally for the live music and the DJs that play here. There are long picnic tables outside, and you can just squeeze in wherever there's room. It can get very busy, especially during major sporting events.

2153 Frederick Douglass Blvd, www.harlemtavern.com, tel. 212-866-4500, Sun-Thu noon-2am, Fri-Sat noon-4am, $22, B, C, 2 & 3 trains to 116 St

SHOPPING

❷ On **Columbus Avenue between West 68th and West 72nd streets** there are a variety of upscale boutiques that are worth checking out, if for nothing else than to gawk at the beautiful objects on display. Among the stores you'll find here are Sean, SEE, Gas Bijoux, Athleta, Kate Spade, Maje, and Monaco.

Columbus Ave, between W 68th and W 72nd streets, 1 train to 66th Street, 1, 2, 3, B & C trains to 72 St

㉝ Silvana is a colorful shop and café in one. The vibe here is a mix of African and Israeli, and they sell a variety of thoughtful objects, including everything from cards and vases to jewelry, handmade clothes, and other odds and ends. You can also come here for coffee, breakfast, lunch, or dinner, and every evening there is live music in the bar downstairs.

300 W 116 St, www.silvana-nyc.com, tel. 646-692-4935, daily 8am-10pm (bar daily 4pm-4am), B & C trains to 116 St

MORE TO EXPLORE

⓭ Riverside Park is located on the west side of Manhattan. It stretches about 4 miles (6.5 km), from 155th Street in the north to 59th Street in the south. This is a good alternative to Central Park if you are looking for someplace green to relax—it's also where residents of the Upper West Side and Harlem come. Here you can go for long walks and bike rides while enjoying a great view of the Hudson. Around 91st Street there is a local garden—the People's Garden—which is wonderfully maintained by 40 diligent volunteers.

W 91st St, www.nycgovparks.org, sunrise to sunset, 1, 2 & 3 trains to 96 St

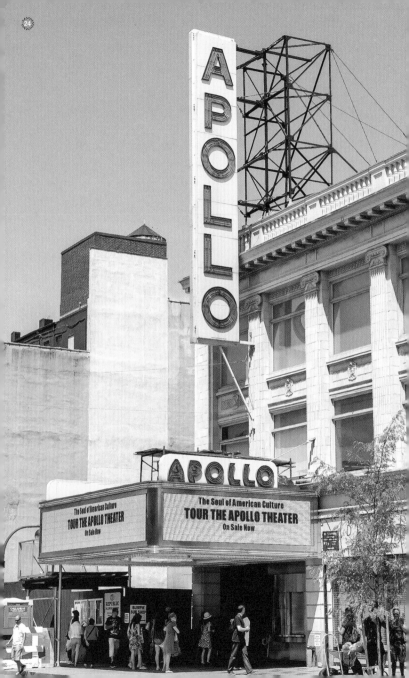

㉓ **Morningside Park** is beautifully kept oasis of calm—the perfect spot for a break. It is especially nice in the morning when you can watch the sun rise over the hill. Take the stairs down and enjoy the excellent view of the park and of Harlem. There is a farmer's market in the park all day on Saturdays, where you can shop for fresh fruits and vegetables. There are also regular music performances.

From W 110th to W 123rd streets, between Manhattan Ave, Morningside Ave, and Morningside Dr, www.morningsidepark.org, tel. 212-937-3883, daily, A & B trains to 116 St

㉔ **Apollo Theater** is a place where stars are born. Ella Fitzgerald, James Brown, Michael Jackson, D'Angelo, and Lauryn Hill have all performed here. Others have made their debut here during the famous Wednesday night "Amateur Night," which is a true one-of-a-kind experience. The theater also has its own Walk of Fame.

253 W 125th St, www.apollotheater.org, tel. 212-531-5300, tickets sold Mon-Fri 10am-6pm, Sat noon-5pm, prices vary, A, B, C, D, 2 & 3 trains to 125 St

㉖ There's nothing more American, New York, or even more typical of Harlem than jazz! Jazz lives in this borough, and the **National Jazz Museum in Harlem** knows to highlight it all. An interesting and not too big of a collection gives you a great overview of jazz in New York.

58 W 129th St, ground floor, jazzmuseuminharlem.org, tel. 212-348-8300, Thu-Mon 11am-5pm, $10 (voluntary donation), 2 & 3 trains to 125 St

㉞ For beautiful, untouched nature, head to **the Ravine** in Central Park. Fallen trees here are left where they are, as long as they don't block the walking paths, and there are dozens of types of birds, plants, and flowers that you wouldn't expect to find in a place like New York City. **The Loch,** an impressive waterfall, is also located here.

W 110th St, Park North between 106th and 102nd streets, www.centralparknyc.org, open daily 6am-1am, 6 train to 103 St

WILLIAMSBURG

ABOUT THE WALK

This surprising walk to and through the hip Williamsburg neighborhood is for those who know how to appreciate the good things in life. The route will bring you past countless restaurants, cafés, and unique vintage stores where young New Yorkers come to eat and shop. The vibe here is creative and dynamic, and the low buildings give a completely different perspective of the city than when you walk through the streets of Manhattan.

THE NEIGHBORHOODS

Until the late 19th century, **Williamsburg,** in Brooklyn, was primarily a place where the Manhattan elite came for a weekend away from the big city. It didn't officially become part of New York City until 1898, when Brooklyn became a borough of New York City. The completion of the **Williamsburg Bridge** in 1903 made it possible for the average person to travel across the East River. Newly arrived immigrants and those escaping the packed tenement buildings of the Lower East Side soon flooded into Brooklyn, and Williamsburg became one of the most densely populated neighborhoods in the city.

Brooklyn has always been a melting pot of cultures, and this is still very visible in Williamsburg today. Williamsburg originated in what is now **South Williamsburg.** Here there are significant populations of Hasidic Jews, Puerto Ricans, and Dominicans. The north of Williamsburg, known as the **North Side,** is home to large Polish and Italian communities.

Recent years have seen many young Manhattanites making the move across the water, and Williamsburg has become one of Brooklyn's hippest, most popular neighborhoods. While artists and creative types were the trailblazers of this new generation of residents, today there is also a growing influx of young professionals who live and work in (luxury) apartments on the waterfront with a view of the city. These new buildings are tucked between old, industrial structures such as the Domino Factory, which you can sail past on the ferry.

In creative Williamsburg, street art is a way of life. Nowhere else in New York City will you find so many murals, stickers, and stencils on walls, building facades, lampposts, doors, mailboxes, curbs, or just about anywhere. Those who pay attention will notice the recurring work of certain artists throughout the neighborhood. If you haven't been to Williamsburg, you haven't really seen New York City.

SHORT ON TIME? HERE ARE THE HIGHLIGHTS:

7 FETTE SAU + 15 MAST BROTHERS CHOCOLATE + 31 MUSIC HALL OF WILLIAMSBURG + 32 ARTISTS & FLEAS + 34 SMORGASBURG

TIPS

// Afternoons are a great time to visit Williamsburg
// Come here for happy hour on the weekend
// Williamsburg is easy to get to on the L train or by bicycle

WILLIAMSBURG

WALK 6 DESCRIPTION (approx. 5.3 mi/8.5 km)

Start in Manhattan and walk across the Williamsburg Bridge ❶, remembering to look back from time to time to check out the amazing view of the city. Be sure to watch out for cyclists. Once on the Williamsburg side, take the ramp down and make a right. Cross the street and go left to visit an art gallery ❷. Then walk back to where you came from, go under the bridge and continue on Bedford Avenue, where there are nice shops and good places to get breakfast and coffee ❸ ❹. Turn right on South 1st Street, where you'll find a stylish barber ❺. Take a left on Havemeyer Street. To the right on Metropolitan Avenue there is a small museum about the city ❻, a restaurant ❼, and a music stage ❽ in front of you. Go left and left again on Roebling Street, right on Fillmore Place, left on Driggs Avenue ❾ ❿, and right on Grand Street for more shopping ⓫. Make a right on Berry Street and then left on Metropolitan Ave. Then turn right on Wythe Avenue for more shopping ⓬ ⓭. Take a right on North 4th Street for special ice cream ⓮. Walk back and take a left on North 3rd Street for the famous Mast Brothers chocolate bars ⓯. Then turn left on Berry Street for a beer ⓰. Take a right on North 4th Street. Walk until you reach the local shopping street Bedford Avenue, where you can pick up nice cheese and jewelry ⓱ ⓲. Left, on North 5th Street, you'll find vintage clothing and a French bistro ⓳ ⓴. Continue along Bedford Avenue and turn left on North 6th Street for a good coffeehouse ㉑. You can also reserve a table for the evening ㉒. Go right on Wythe Avenue and pick up a yummy sandwich ㉓ and hot sauce ㉔. Take North 8th Street to The Bedford ㉕ where you can eat in an old garage. Turn left on North 11th Street, then right, and then left to North 12th Street for beer tasting ㉖. Head back to Berry Street and walk to Nassau Avenue to listen to the radio ㉗ and play Jenga ㉘. Go back and take a right on North 14th Street and go bowling ㉙. On Wythe Avenue take a left for a design café ㉚. Go right on 10th Street and left on Kent Avenue. Walk all the way to North 6th Street and take a left for entertainment ㉛. Then turn left twice for a creative market ㉜. On the other side of Kent Avenue is the East River Park, the Smorgasburg food trucks, and the ferry back to Manhattan ㉝ ㉞ ㉟.

SIGHTS & ATTRACTIONS

❶ The **Williamsburg Bridge** connects Manhattan and Williamsburg. It is used by cars and trucks, but you can also cross by bicycle or on foot. The view of eastern Manhattan from the Williamsburg side is amazing, and since cyclists and pedestrians are separated from the rest of traffic, getting to the other side is both safe and pleasant.
Corner of Delancey St and Clinton St, J, M & Z trains to Essex Street, F train to Delancey Street, B & D trains to Grand St

❷ Kings County Savings Bank previously stood on the spot where the **Williamsburg Art & Historical Center** is now located. This is the best-known gallery in the neighborhood. Exhibits here change regularly and include everything from paintings and sculptures to installations and modern art. The center exhibits the work of both American and international artists.
135 Broadway, www.wahcenter.net, tel. 718-486-6012, Fri-Sun noon-6pm, free, J, M & Z trains to Marcy Av, L train to Bedford Av

❻ The tiny **City Reliquary Museum** is definitely not your average museum. It is packed with rare artifacts that relate to the history of New York City. There is a replica of the Bay Ridge Barbershop, which operated in Brooklyn for 50 years, as well as a collection of items from the 1964 World's Fair held in New York. The gift shop has fun, interesting items by local artists.
370 Metropolitan Ave, www.cityreliquary.org, tel. 718-782-4842, Thu-Sun noon-6pm, $5 donation, L train to Lorimer St, G train to Metropolitan Av

㉝ With its spectacular view looking out over the river onto Manhattan, the **East River State Park** is the perfect place to come to relax and maybe take a few photos. On Saturdays, when the Smorgasburg market takes place here, the park is also a great place to come for fresh, tasty snacks and treats.
3236 N 8th St, www.nysparks.com, daily 9am-sunset, East River Ferry to North 6th Street/North Williamsburg, L train to Bedford Av

FOOD & DRINK

❹ Enter the **Rabbithole Restaurant** and you'll find yourself in the bar/café area where you can get yummy Stumptown coffee. Order a scone or muffin—baked by Ms. Rabbithole herself—to go with it. The restaurant is in the rear, and the garden out back is a fabulous green setting where you can sit and enjoy a meal.

352 Bedford Ave, www.rabbitholerestaurant.com, tel. 718-782-0910, daily 9am-5pm and 6pm-11pm, $18, L train to Bedford Av, J, M & Z trains to Marcy Av

❼ **Fette Sau** is a mandatory destination for all meat lovers. Located in an old garage, the restaurant serves delicious barbeque all year. Come find a spot at one of the long tables here, or when the weather is nice, enjoy a seat outside. Be sure to get here early, though, or you'll have to wait in line. By the time you get a seat, your favorite cut of meat may already be gone.

354 Metropolitan Ave, www.fettesaubbq.com, tel. 718-963-3404, Mon 5pm-11pm, Tue-Sun noon-11pm, $18, L train to Lorimer St, G train to Metropolitan Av

⓮ **Republic of Booza** is the first shop in the United States to sell booza, and it's definitely worth a visit. Booza ice cream was invented about 500 years ago in the eastern Mediterranean. Ice cream as we know it, is based on booza, but booza is more elastic and creamier and has a richer taste. The recipe and technique may be ancient, but the shop has a hypermodern, almost Japanese interior. And, besides the traditional flavors, they experiment with all different kinds of ingredients, such as Chinese pepper combined with Oreo cookies.

76 N 4th St, www.republicofbooza.com, tel. 718-302-5000, Sun-Thu noon-11pm, Fri-Sat noon-midnight, G train to Greenpoint Av

⓰ Who knew New York was once the home to a large group of German immigrants? And they made their mark on the food and drinking culture of the city. **Radegast Hall & Biergarten** started pouring beer only in 2007, but New Yorkers feel right at home in this cozy space where mugs of beer and big sausages are served without any qualms.

113 N 3rd St, www.radegasthall.com, tel. 718-963-3973, Mon noon-4am, Tue-Fri noon-2am, Sat-Sun 11am-4am, *wursts* or burgers from $13, L train to Bedford Av, East River Ferry to North 6th St/North Williamsburg

㉟ **Juliette** is a charming French bistro in the homey neighborhood of Williamsburg. The imported classic interior comes straight from Paris, and the Parisian menu, with French onion soup *gratinée* and *escargot maison*, makes the European vibe complete.

135 N 5th St, www.juliettewilliamsburg.com, tel. 718-388-9222, Sun-Thu 10:30am-11pm, Fri-Sat 10:30am-midnight, $18, L train to Bedford Av

㉑ **Partners Coffee** began as Toby's Estate, which specialized in Australian coffees. The successful café originated in Australia years ago when owner, Toby Smith, started roasting his own coffee. Years later, the company opened its first American location in Williamsburg. Partners still offers "short blacks" and "flat whites" as well as small-batch roasted beans, breakfast, and lunch.

125 N 6th St, https://www.partnerscoffee.com , tel. 347-586-0063, daily 6:30am-6pm, coffees from $4, L train to Bedford Av, East River Ferry to North 6th St/North Williamsburg

㉒ Writers, artists, and other creative souls from the neighborhood like to slide into the old-style booths at **Sweetwater** and enjoy a nice dinner. This American bistro serves up dishes from a variety of areas. On warm summer evenings, the terrace is a perfect place to linger until late into the night.

105 N 6th St, www.sweetwaterny.com, tel. 718-963-0608, Mon-Fri 11am-midnight, Sat-Sun 10:30am-midnight, $20, L train to Bedford Av, East River Ferry to North 6th St/North Williamsburg

㉓ **Bakeri** is a small bakery and café with a bohemian vibe. Enjoy delicious, freshly baked bread, pastries, and cookies in a charming space full of thoughtful details, such as a collage of picture frames, flowers, and beautiful handwritten cards. Of course, they also serve coffee to go along with all of the delicious treats. A house favorite is the Norwegian *skolebrød*, a type of sweet bun.

150 Wythe Ave, www.bakeribrooklyn.com, tel. 718-388-8037, Mon-Fri 7am-7pm, Sat-Sun 8am-7pm, $8, L train to Bedford Av, East River Ferry to North 6th St/North Williamsburg

25 Located in a former garage, **The Bedford** is a restaurant with a rustic, vintage appearance. The beautiful corner building with a terrace is a great place for a relaxed night out. The menu includes classic dishes with a twist, such as the Bedford Burger. Have you already eaten? Then a night at the bar may be ideal.
110 Bedford Ave, www.thebedfordonbedford.com, tel. 718-599-7588, Mon-Thu & Sun 11am-2am, Fri-Sat 11am-4am, $21, L train to Bedford Av, East River Ferry to North 6th St/North Williamsburg

28 **Spritzenhaus 33** is a cool bar that boasts a large selection of beer and snacks and has Jenga games on every wooden table. When the weather permits, they open the glass walls to the outside, and you can drink your beer and play a game of Jenga while enjoying the outdoors. Here's to hoping it won't be too windy!
33 Nassau Ave, www.spritzenhaus33.com, tel. 347-987-4632, Mon-Thu 3pm-1am, Fri-Sun noon-4am, $10, G train to Nassau Av

30 Here's another former garage that has been reinvented with a new culinary function—this time as a design café. In the summer the doors to **Kinfolk** stand wide open, giving the wonderful sensation of being outdoors while inside. The centerpiece at Kinfolk is the black walnut bar. In the morning the café is open for coffee, and in the evening, you can come here for beer. Next to the garage is the Kinfolk men's clothing store, and it's worth taking a peek inside.
90 Wythe Ave, www.kinfolklife.com, Mon-Fri 8:30am-late, Sat-Sun 11am-late, $10, L train to Bedford Av, East River Ferry to North 6th St/North Williamsburg

SHOPPING

3 Come to **Fanaberie** for one-of-a-kind, colorful clothes you can be sure no one else back home will be wearing. According to the owner, the items in the store are "eclectic"—and they are also "pleasantly surprising." The unique prints are sure to win you some admiring looks, and the jewelry and bags are all reasonably priced.
339 Bedford Ave, www.fanaberienyc.com, tel. 347-599-0177, Mon-Wed 10:30am-7:30pm, Fri 10:30am-8pm, Sat 10:30am-7pm, Sun 11am-7pm, L train to Bedford Av, J, M & Z trains to Marcy Av

❾ The owner of **Bird** started out as an assistant buyer for Barneys. Today she has her own stores where she sells designer clothes for men and women. The shop also regularly hosts photography and art exhibits.

203 Grand St, www.birdbrooklyn.com, tel. 718-388-1655, Mon & Fri 11am-8pm, Tue-Thu noon-8pm, Sat-Sun 11am-7pm, L train to Bedford Av

❿ **Mociun** is run by an interior designer, which is immediately visible from the store's beautiful, light interior. The space actually looks more like a gallery than a store. Come here for beautiful jewelry, silk textiles, ceramic accessories, and small works of art for special occasions.

683 Driggs Ave, www.mociun.com, tel. 347-227-8966, Mon-Sun noon-8pm, Sun noon-7pm, L train to Bedford Av

⓫ The German designer behind **Berlyn 65** single-handedly selects the store's collection of unique jewelry, silk cloths, and other little odds and ends. The jewelry is made by local designers, making it all the better. Once inside the shop, you are immediately transported to a place of calm and relaxation.

163 Grand St, www.berlyn65.com, tel. 917-338-7570, Tue-Sat noon-8pm, Sun noon-7pm, L train to Bedford Av, M, J & Z trains to Marcy Av

⓬ Surf culture is surprisingly popular in New York City. Come to **Pilgrim Surf** for surf supplies as well as stylish men's street-style clothes. They have a great sneaker collection, for example. They also sell lifestyle books and accessories.

68 N 3th St, www.pilgrimsurfsupply.com, tel. 718-218-7456, Mon-Fri noon-8pm, Sat-Sun 11am-7pm, L train to Bedford Av

⓭ Mociun and Isa Baggu originally opened **Baggu** as a pop-up store, but it was such a success that they decided to turn it into a permanent shop. Their bags are playful, colorful, and minimalist and are available in all sizes and shapes. Even if you already have lots of bags, there's always a place for a Baggu bag in your closet.

242 Wythe Ave #4, entrance on N 3rd St, www.baggu.com, daily 11am-7pm, L train to Bedford Av

3.

Fermentation
3-6 days.

4.

SUN

Cacao

d to Brooklyn
the world.

beans ferment naturally
in wooden boxes & covered
in plantain leaves.

Beans are Sun

6.

Stone Ground

granite
wheels

7.

$7

Cho

Roasting

beans are roasted
delicately in ovens.

after shells are
removed, the beans
are ground for 3 days

R

Single Origin
San Martin

Vanilla
& Smoke

Crown
Maple

Maine
Sea Salt

Cocoa Nibs

Stumptown
Coffee

Serrano

Hazelnut

MAST BROTHERS CHOCOLATE

MAST BROTHERS CHOCOLATE

MAST BROTHERS CHOCOLATE

MAST BROTHERS CHOCOLATE

15 The local chocolate maker **Mast Brothers Chocolate** sells beautifully packaged bars of chocolate in flavors such as serrano pepper, Brooklyn blend, and Stumptown coffee. Step inside to smell the delicious aroma and sample one of the many types of chocolate they offer.

111 N 3rd St, www.mastchocolate.com, tel. 718-388-2625, Sat 10am-7pm, Sun 10am-5m, L train to Bedford Av, East River Ferry to North 6th St/North Williamsburg

17 This old-fashioned cheese shop is a rare gem in New York City. The **Bedford Cheese Shop** sells cheeses from all around the world, and it goes without saying, this is the place for a grilled cheese sandwich if you manage to stop by here at lunchtime.

229 Bedford Ave, www.bedfordcheeseshop.com, tel. 718-395-9943, Mon-Sat 8am-9pm, Sun 8am-8pm, L train to Bedford Av, East River Ferry to North 6th St/North Williamsburg

18 **Catbird** is a small store full of old-fashioned toys, cards, knickknacks, and hair accessories. Above all, however, the store's specialty is its great collection of locally designed jewelry.

219 Bedford Ave, www.catbirdnyc.com, tel. 718-599-3457, Mon-Sat noon-8pm, Sun noon-6pm, L train to Bedford Av, East River Ferry to North 6th St/North Williamsburg

19 Audible from all the way down the street, the music at **Awoke Vintage** draws in all the neighborhood hipsters. Of course, besides the music, people come here for the unique secondhand clothes, including everything from leather jackets and shorts to fun dresses. With any luck, you might just find that special item you've always been looking for.

132 N 5th St, www.awokevintage.com, tel. 718-387-3130, daily 10am-9pm, L train to Bedford Av, East River Ferry to North 6th St/North Williamsburg

24 If you love spicy food, you have to visit the **Heatonist.** This Japanese-style shop sells much more than hot sauces and oils from all over the world. Where else can you buy a hot sauce gift set?

121 Wythe Ave, www.heatonist.com, tel. 718-599-0838, daily noon-8pm, L train to Bedford Av

32 **Artists & Fleas** is open every Saturday and Sunday. Come to this covered market for antiques, vintage items, art, photography, clothes, jewelry, and accessories. Everything is sold by the artists themselves.

70 N 7th St, www.artistsandfleas.com, Sat-Sun 10am-7pm, L train to Bedford Av, G train to Metropolitan Av, East River Ferry to North 6th St/North Williamsburg

MORE TO EXPLORE

5 Williamsburg is known as a hipster mecca and often associated with men with beards and man buns. At **Filthy Rich Barbershop** they not only give you a trendy haircut, they also style famous rappers like Big Sean and Flo Rida. It's been an institution since 2006.

148 Havemeyer St, www.filthyrichbarbershop.com, tel. 718-396-3300, Mon-Thu & Sat 11am-8pm, Fri 11am-7pm, Sun noon-6pm, from $40, G train to Metropolitan Av

8 The **Knitting Factory** is a well-known name on the New York music scene. Just like The Bitter End and Arlene's Grocery, this place has given a podium to (then) unknown punk, pop, rock, and funk legends. Maybe the next Nirvana will be on stage during your visit!

361 Metropolitan Ave, bk.knittingfactory.com, tel. 347-529-6696, daily 7:30pm-11pm, $12, G train to Metropolitan Av

26 During the week, **Brooklyn Brewery** is only open for tours. However, starting Friday afternoon at 5pm a line begins to form in front of the door as people wait for the tasting room to open. The fantastic beers are inexpensive by NYC standards, and though they don't offer much in terms of food here, they don't mind if patrons have a pizza delivered.

79 N 11th St, www.brooklynbrewery.com, tel. 718-486-7422, Mon-Thu 5pm (tours only), Fri 6pm-11pm, Sat noon-8pm (free tours each hour until 5pm), beer coins $5, L train to Bedford Av, G train to Nassau Av, East River Ferry to North 6th St/North Williamsburg

27 At first glance you might think **The Lot Radio** is a public watering hole but look again and you'll see it looks more like a radio station run by squatters. Actually, The Lot Radio is a radio station that broadcasts 24/7 from an empty building lot in New York. They happen to have some chairs and tables standing around, and that's what makes The Lot Radio the local hotspot to sit in the sun and drink a beer with friends while listening to live radio.

17 Nassau Ave, www.thelotradio.com, Mon-Fri 8am-midnight, Sat-Sun 1am-midnight, G train to Nassau Av

29 In Williamsburg people appreciate a beer and a good game of bowling. The neighborhood has three bowling alleys, and **The Gutter** is one of them. Although it only opened in 2007, once you step inside, you'll feel you're back in the 1950s. If you have to wait for a lane here, pass the time while playing an old-fashioned boardgame.

200 N 14th St, www.thegutterbrooklyn.com, tel. 718-387-3585, Mon-Thu 4pm-4am, Fri 2pm-4am, Sat-Sun noon-4am, from $40 per hour, shoe rental $3 (cash only), G train to Nassau Av, L train to Bedford Av, East River Ferry to North 6th St/North Williamsburg

BLUEBERRY STRAWBERRY TRIPLE BERRY

POP ART → JAM TARTS

Every evening at the **Music Hall of Williamsburg** you can catch performances by little-known bands. There is a great view of the stage from anywhere in the house, and the sound is amazing! Buy your tickets online, at the door, or from a box office.

66 N 6th St, www.musichallofwilliamsburg.com, tel. 718-486-5400, Williamsburg box office Sat 11am-6pm, Manhattan box office (at Mercury Lounge, 6 Delancey St) Mon-Sat noon-7pm, L train to Bedford Av, East River Ferry to North 6th St/North Williamsburg

Every Saturday some 50 venders gather at the **Smorgasburg** market to sell their delicious homemade snacks. Think hamburgers, sandwiches, ice cream, coffee, tea, and lemonade. There are also vendors selling clothes, jewelry, and accessories. On Sunday the market moves to Brooklyn Bridge Park Pier 5, and during the winter months it is inside at 80 North 5th Street all weekend long.

90 Kent Ave, at N 7th St, www.smorgasburg.com, Sat 11am-6pm, East River Ferry to North 6th St/North Williamsburg

Instead of heading back to Manhattan underground, you can also take the **East River Ferry.** Head north and get off at 34th Street or take a boat south to Pier 11 at Wall Street. New York City is always an impressive sight to see from the water.

N 6th St on the waterfront, www.ferry.nyc/routes-and-schedules/route/east-river, tel. 844-469-3377, daily, check website for times, single journey $4, L train to Bedford Av

WITH MORE TIME

The walks in this book will take you to most of the city's main highlights. Of course, there are still many places worth visiting and things worth seeing that have not been included. We have listed them below. Note that not all of these places are easily accessible by foot from in town, but you can get to them all using public transportation.

Ⓐ Since 1952 the **United Nations** headquarters has stood on this spot. The buildings' simple geometric shapes, glass walls, and lack of cultural references are characteristic of the international style in which it was built. The Visitors Centre is free and regularly hosts interesting exhibits. It is also possible to take a guided tour.
1st Ave, between 42nd and 48th streets, https://visit.un.org, tel. 212-963-8687, Mon-Fri 9am-4:30pm (guided tour), Sat-Sun 10am-4:30pm, $18, S, 4, 5, 6 & 7 trains to Grand Central-42 St

Ⓑ The **Brooklyn Museum** is one of the country's oldest and largest museums. Its permanent collection includes a range of objects, including art from various world cultures as well as paintings, sculptures, and much more. However, it's the museum's temporary exhibitions in particular that draw so many visitors to this stately building, which dates back to 1895. It's not possible to see everything here in one day, so you'll have to make some choices.
200 Eastern Pkwy, www.brooklynmuseum.org, tel. 718-638-5000, Wed & Fri-Sun 11am-6pm, Thu 11am-10pm, 1st Sat of the month 11am-11pm, $16, 2 & 3 trains to Eastern Pkwy-Bklyn Museum

Ⓒ Although officially still in Manhattan, the **Met Cloisters**—perched on a hilltop above the city—gives the impression that you're far away from the urban bustle of the city. The museum is a branch of the Metropolitan Museum of Art dedicated to medieval art.
99 Margaret Corbin Dr, www.metmuseum.org/visit/plan-your-visit/met-cloisters, tel. 212-923-3700, daily Mar-Oct 10am-5:15pm, Nov-Feb 10am-4:45pm,
$25 (can be used the same day at the Met), A train to 190 St, then bus M4 to Ft Tryon Park/Café Lot

Ⓓ The **Pieter Claesen Wyckoff House** dates back to 1652 and is therefore the oldest Dutch building in New York City and the surrounding area. The small museum housed here today tells about daily Dutch life in New York at that time centuries ago.

5816 Clarendon Rd, www.wyckoffmuseum.org, tel. 718-629-5400, Fri-Sat noon-4pm, $5 (museum visits by tour only), B & Q trains to Newkirk Plaza or 2 & 5 trains to Newkirk Av, then bus B8 to Beverly Rd/Ralph Av

Ⓔ Walk along the romantic **Brooklyn Heights Promenade** and take in the famous view of the East River, the Statue of Liberty, and the Brooklyn Bridge. Since the promenade opened in 1950, countless photographers and filmmakers have focused their cameras in this direction both by day and by night.

Brooklyn Heights Promenade, entrance from Middaugh or Cranberry St, A & C trains to High St, 2 & 3 trains to Clark St

Ⓕ When the makers of Central Park were asked to design a park for Brooklyn, they designed **Prospect Park.** At the point is **Grand Army Plaza,** with the Soldiers & Sailors Monument, which forms the entrance to the park. Around this plaza you'll find the Brooklyn Library, the Brooklyn Museum, and Flatbush Avenue that separates Prospect Park from the Brooklyn Botanical Garden. It's a place with lots to do.

Flatbush Ave, www.nycgovparks.org/parks/B073, tel. 718-965-8999, Q train to Parkside Av

Ⓖ The **Hudson River Park** stretches some 4.5 miles from Battery Park to 57th Street. The park is full of activity and offers lots to do. Come here for kayaking, ice skating, and playing in the playgrounds. There are also tennis courts and boat clubs. Throughout the year many events are organized in the park. Tip: there's a scenic 2-mile walking route along the Hudson River that starts at Battery Park. Afterward, have a refreshing drink at Pier 45. In the summer the grassy field fills up with sunbathers—there are even outside showers to help you cool down when it gets too hot.

Battery Park to 57th St, www.hudsonriverpark.org, free, 1 train to Whitehall St, 5 train to Bowling Green

Ⓗ The **Museum at FIT (Fashion Institute of Technology)** is a slice of heaven on earth for fashion lovers. It is home to the world's largest collection of garments and accessories and includes items of fashion and haute couture from the 18th century to the present. There are also regular exhibitions from big names in the fashion world. During New York Fashion Week a visit here is a must—who knows, maybe you'll even run into a famous designer or blogger.

7th Ave, at W 27th St, www.fitnyc.edu/museum.asp, tel. 212-217-4558, Tue-Fri noon-8pm, Sat 10am-5pm, free, 1, N & R trains to 28 St

Ⓘ New York has a number of great **beaches.** Some are free, while others are not because they also have lifeguards. The large Rockaway Beach in Queens is the only beach in New York City where surfing is permitted, and it is accessible by subway and with the NYC Beach Bus (www.nycbeachbus .com). Long Beach, on Long Island, is about 3 miles long, and you can walk right out of the train station and onto the sand. Brooklyn's Coney Island has a wonderful boardwalk and amusement park, and is easily accessible by subway. Manhattan Beach, also in Brooklyn, is a small, family beach next to Brighton Beach, and people come here for picnics and to barbeque by the water. Beach season in New York officially opens each year on Memorial Day weekend in late May and goes until Labor Day in early September.

Rockaway Beach between Beach 9th St & Beach 149th St, Queens, www.nycgovparks.org, daily 6am-9pm, boardwalk 6am-10pm, free, A train to Broad Channel, S train to Rockaway Park-Beach 116 St

(J) End the day with a stop at the **Upright Citizens Brigade Theatre,** a comedy club for stand-up and improv. Every evening you can catch shows from the funniest and most creative comedians in the business. Tickets are usually around $10 or less, and on Sunday nights the 9:30 shows are free.

307 W 26th St, www.ucbtheatre.com, tel. 212-366-9176, daily, see website for times and shows, tickets from $5, Sun 9:30pm free, 1 train to 28 St, A & C trains to 23 St

(K) **Governors Island** is a small island less than half a mile off the coast of lower Manhattan. For nearly 200 years Governors Island was not accessible to civilians, but since 2006 it has been open to the public. Ferries shuttle visitors across the water to this former army base in just seven minutes. Come here for the military history, for a festival, to picnic near the Statue of Liberty, or simply to enjoy the greenery and the awesome view of the NYC skyline. A good way to explore the island is by bike—bring your own on the ferry or rent one at Bike and Roll when you arrive.

Governors Island, www.govisland.com, from May 23 to Sep 27, Mon-Fri 10am-6pm, Sat-Sun 10am-7pm, ferry ticket $2, 1 train to South Ferry, 4 & 5 trains to Bowling Green, R train to Whitehall St-South Ferry

NIGHTLIFE

New York City and nightlife are inseparable concepts. Whatever scene you're into—clubs, comedy shows, jazz, alternative music, theater, or film—there's plenty of everything to keep you entertained. Even if you want to try and cram it all into one night, NYC won't disappoint.

You have to be 21 to get into most bars and clubs, so don't forget to bring your ID when you go out because you are sure to be carded. Many clubs and bars and even restaurants have a dress code. Often you can find that information on their websites, but it's safe to assume that you won't be allowed in a club or rooftop terrace wearing flip-flops or hiking shoes. At some restaurants men must wear a jacket. A few places (think 21 Club) have beautiful Armani jackets you can rent in case you forgot yours.

HOTELS

A good bed, a tasty breakfast, and a nice interior—these are all ingredients for a pleasant hotel stay. Equally as important, however, is the location. A hotel is really good only if you can walk out of the lobby and straight into the bustling city.

New York City has more than 100,000 hotel rooms to choose from. The options range from the usual big chains to intimate boutique hotels to penthouse suites.

If you want to be right in the thick of things, then Midtown Manhattan is the place to stay. The modern Ace Hotel, for example, is within walking distance of many sights and attractions. Equally central but in a slightly calmer area downtown, East Village Bed and Coffee is a popular guesthouse. This small B&B in the hip East Village is close to vintage stores, coffee shops, restaurants, and bars. Not your first time in NYC? Then maybe you want to consider accommodations in Brooklyn, such as at the comfortable New York Loft Hostel, which is conveniently located near the L train that takes you into Williamsburg or across the river into Manhattan.

INDEX

INDEX

MOON
NEW YORK CITY WALKS
SECOND EDITION

AVALON TRAVEL
Hachette Book Group
1700 Fourth Street
Berkeley, CA 94710, USA
www.moon.com

ISBN 978-1-64049-789-4
Concept & Original Publication
"time to momo New York"
© 2020 by mo'media.
All rights reserved.

time to momo

MO' MEDIA

Text and Walks
Ted Steinebach

Translation
Cindi Heller

Design
Studio 100% &
Oranje Vormgevers

Photography
Marjolein den Hartog,
René Clement, Wendy Mahieu

Project Editor
Sophie Kreuze

AVALON TRAVEL

Project Editor
Lori Hobkirk

Typesetting
Cynthia Young

Copy Editor
Lori Hobkirk

Proofreader
Sandy Chapman

Cover Design
Faceout Studio, Jeff Miller

Printed in China by
RR Donnelley
First US printing,
April 2020

Trips to Remember

GALÁPAGOS ISLANDS

ANGKOR WAT

BELIZE

COSTA RICA

FIJI

JAPAN

MACHU PICCHU

MOROCCO

NEW ZEALAND

PATAGONIA

VIETNAM

Grand Adventure

APPALACHIAN TRAIL

PACIFIC COAST HIGHWAY

USA NATIONAL PARKS

THE COMPLETE GUIDE TO ALL
59 PARKS

MOON.COM
@MOONGUIDES

Embark on an epic journey along the historic Camino de Santiago, stroll the most popular European cities, or chase the northern lights in Norway with Moon Travel Guides!

GO BIG AND GO BEYOND!
These savvy city guides include strategies to help you see the top sights and find adventure beyond the tourist crowds.

OR TAKE THINGS ONE STEP AT A TIME